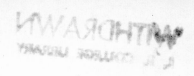

Columbia University

STUDIES IN ROMANCE PHILOLOGY AND LITERATURE

CHAUCER'S INDEBTEDNESS TO GUIDO DELLE COLONNE

THE INDEBTEDNESS OF CHAUCER'S TROILUS AND CRISEYDE TO GUIDO DELLE COLONNE'S HISTORIA TROJANA

BY

GEORGE L. HAMILTON, A.M.

SOMETIME FELLOW IN COLUMBIA UNIVERSITY
PROFESSOR OF ROMANCE LANGUAGES IN TRINITY COLLEGE
NORTH CAROLINA

AMS PRESS, INC.
NEW YORK
1966

PREFACE

THE following study is a dissertation offered in the spring of 1900 to the Faculty of Philosophy of Columbia University, in fulfilment of one of the requirements for the degree of Doctor of Philosophy. My original plan was to make an investigation of Chaucer's indebtedness to the French and Latin writers who were his predecessors in telling the story of Troilus and Criseyde, but owing to the fact that Joly's edition of the *Roman de Troie* is so very incomplete and uncritical, I confined my study to the work of Guido, citing from the French poem only when it was necessary to quote illustrative parallel passages. I have used the 1486 Strasburg edition of the *Historia Trojana*, but I have been able to collate the passages cited with the readings in the

best and oldest manuscripts of the work in
the Bibliothèque Nationale and the British
Museum, without, however, finding cause to
make changes which were essential.

Studies made subsequent to the writing of
this dissertation, upon the relations between
versions of Benoit's work and the plagiary of
Guido, may lead me, at a later date, to mod-
ify certain statements.

I desire to thank Professor Henry A. Todd
for his kindness and care in reading over, and
giving helpful criticism on, the manuscript of
this book.

CHAUCER'S INDEBTEDNESS TO GUIDO DELLE COLONNE

CHAUCER'S INDEBTEDNESS TO GUIDO DELLE COLONNE

ONE of the most discussed of literary problems is that of the sources of Chaucer's *Troilus and Criseyde*, owing, among other causes, to the author's own statements of the case. Twice in the poem he cites the name of the writer who he would have us think was the author of the book from which he draws his narrative : —

"Myn autour called Lollius" (I. 394),
" As telleth Lollius " (V. 1653),

and whom he elsewhere enumerates with those who have written about Trojan matters : —

" And by him stood, withouten lees,
Ful wonder hye on a pileer,

> Of yren, he, the gret Omeer ;
> And with him Dares and Tytus
> Before, and eek he, Lollius,
> And Guido eek de Columpnis,
> And English Ganfride eek, y-wis,
> And ech of these, as have I joye,
> Was besy for to bere up Troye." [1]

It is only the task of a translator that he undertakes; he has rendered the story out of the original text

> "in swich English as he can," [2]

and attempts nothing beyond : —

> " O lady myn, that called art Cleo,
> Thou be my speed fro this forth, and my muse,
> To ryme wel this book, til I have do ;
> Me nedeth here noon other art to use.
> For-why to every lovere I me excuse,
> That of no sentement I this endyte,

---

[1] *Hous of Fame*, 1464–1472.
[2] *Canterbury Tales*, Group B, 49.   Cf. *L. of G. W.*, A, 85–88.

But out of Latin in my tongue it wryte"
(II. 8–14).[1]

He frequently calls attention to the closeness of the translation he is making of his
original, which he mentions as if it were
his sole authority, whether he refers to the
writer or his work : —

" And of his song nought only the sentence,
    As writ myn autour called Lollius,
    But pleynly, save our tonges difference,

[1] Cf. *L. of G. W.*, A, 264–266 : —

" Hast thou nat mad in English eek the book
    How that Crisseyde Troilus forsook
    In shewinge how that wemen han don mis ? "

But in the second form of the same passage the God of
Love reproaches the poet, as if he had expressed merely
his own " sentement " in that work.   *L. of G. W.*, B, 332–
334 : —

" And of Criseyde thou hast seyd as thee liste ;
    That maketh men to wommen lasse triste
    That ben as trewe as ever was any steel."

In the *Retraction* at the end of the *Persones Tale*, " the
book of Troilus " is the first mentioned in the list " of
my translacions and endytinges of worldly vanitees."
Canterbury Tales, Group I, 1084–1085.

I dar wel sayn, in al that Troilus
Seyde in his song; lo! every word right thus
As I shal seyn; and who-so list it here,
Lo! next this vers, he may it finden here"
    (I. 393–399).

" Wherefore I nil have neither thank ne blame
Of al this werk, but pray yow mekely,
Disblameth me, if any word be lame
For as myn auctor seyde, so seye I.
Eek though I speke of love unfelingly,
No wonder is; for it no-thing of-newe is,
A blind man can-not juggen wel in hewis"
    (II. 15–21).[1]

[1] Cf. *L. of G. W.*, A, 340 : —
    " Or elles sir, for that this man is nyce,
      He may translate a thing in no malyce,
      But for he useth bokes for to make,
      And takth non heed of what matere he take;
      Therfor he wroot the Rose and eek Crisseyde
      Of innocence, and niste what he seyde;
      Or him was boden make thilke tweye
      Of som persone, and durst hit nat with-seye;
      For he hath writen many a book er this,
      He ne hath doon nat so grevously amis
      To translaten that olde clerkes wryten,
      As thogh that he of malyce wolde endyten
      Despyt of love, and had him-self y-wroght."
  Cf. *T. and C.*, III. 1328–1336.

"Myn auctor shal I folwen, if I conne" (II.
49).

"And what she thoughte somwhat shal I wryte,
As to myn auctor listeth for to endyte" (II.
699–700).

"For ther was som epistel hem bitwene,
That wolde, as seyth myn auctor, wel contene
An hondred vers, of which him list not wryte;
(*Var.* Neigh half this book, of which him list
not wryte;)
How sholde I thanne a lyne of it endyte"
(III. 501–504).

"Nought list myn auctor fully to declare,
What that she thoughte whan he seyde so,
That Troilus was out of town y-fare,
As if he seyde ther-of sooth or no" (III.
575–578).

"Though that I tarie a yeer, somtyme I moot
After myn auctor, tellen hir gladnesse,
As wel as I have told hir hevinesse" (III.
1195–1197).

"Thourgh yow have I seyd fully in my song
Th'effect and joye of Troilus servyse,
Al be that ther was som disese among,

As to myn auctor listeth to devyse "[1] (III. 1814–1817).

"And after this the story telleth us " (V. 1037).

" But trewely, the story telleth us " (V. 1051).

And again he is careful to give notice that he is abridging his original: —

" [She] gan a lettre wryte,
Of which to telle in short [2] is myn entente
Th'effect, as fer as I can understonde " (II. 1218–1220).

---

[1] In II. 31–32 : —
" As the story will devyse
How Troilus com to his lady grace."
and V. 1093–1094 : —

" Ne me ne list this sely womman chyde
Ferther than the story wol devyse."

reference is made to the tale as it is found in Chaucer's own narrative, as he took it from his sources.   Cf. *T. and C.*, V. 1772–1776.

[2] On the frequency of this phrase and its equivalents, " shortly to tell," and " shortly to say," in Chaucer's poems, cf. T. R. Lounsbury, *Studies in Chaucer*, 1892, Vol. II. pp. 95–96, 547–548.   In *T. and C.* (III. 548, 1117, 1156 ; V. 1009, 1826), except in the passage cited in the text, such expressions are used as mere *chevilles*.

"But, sooth is, though I can not tellen al,
  As can myn auctor, of his excellence,
  Yet have I seyd, and, god to-forn, I shal
  In every-thing al hoolly his sentence" (III.
    1324–1327).

And yet, as if he did not see the contradiction of his own statements, he is careful to note that he consulted various works in writing his poem : —

"But whan his shame gan somwhat to passe,
  His resons, as I may my rymes holde,
  I yow wol telle, as techen bokes olde" (III.
    89–91).

"Criseyde, which that felte hir thus y-take,
  As writen clerkes in hir bokes olde,
  Right as an aspes leef she gan to quake,
  Whan she him felte hir in his armes folde"
    (III. 1198–1201).

"And trewely, how longe is was bitwene,
  That she for-sook him for this Diomede,
  Ther is non auctor telleth it, I wene.
  Take every man now to his bokes hede;
  He shal no terme finden, out of drede" (V.
    1086–1090).

" For how Criseyde Troilus forsook,
  Or at the leste, how that she was unkinde,
  Mot hennes-forth ben matere of my book,
  As wryten folk thorugh which it is in minde.
  Allas ! that they shulde ever cause finde
  To speke hir harm ; and if they on hir lye,
  Y-wis, hem-self sholde han the vilayne " (IV.
    15–21).

" And treweliche, as writen wel I finde,
  That al this thing was seyd of good entente ;
  And that hir herte trewe was and kinde
  Towardes him, and spak right as she mente,
  And that she starf for wo neigh, whan she
    wente,
  And was in purpos ever to be trewe ;
  Thus writen they that of hir werkes knewe "
    (IV. 1415–1421).

" Lo, trewely, they writen that hir syen,
  That Paradys stood formed in hir yen " (V.
    816–817).

" I finde eek in the stories elles-where " (V.
  1044).

" In alle nedes, for the tounes werre,
  He was, and ay the firste in armes dight ;

And certeynly, but-if that bokes erre,
Save Ector, most y-drad of any wight " (III.
1772–1775).

" And trewely, as men in bokes rede " (V. 19).

" This Diomede, as bokes us declare " (V. 799).

" For these bokes wol me shende " (V. 1060).

" For whom, as olde bokes tellen us,
Was maad swich wo, that tonge it may not
telle " (V. 1562–1563).

" In many cruel batayle, out of drede,
Of Troilus, this ilke noble knight,
As men may in these olde bokes rede,
Was sene his knighthod and his grete might "
(V. 1751–1754).

" Ye may hir gilt in othere bokes see " (V.
1776).

The three passages, —

" And certainly in story it is y-founde " (V.
834),

" But certeyn is, to purpos for to go,
That in this whyle, as writen is in geste,
He say his lady som-tyme; and also
She with him spak " (III. 449–451),

" And ofte tyme, I finde that they mette
  With blody strokes and with wordes grete,
  Assayinge how hir speres weren whette ;
  And god it woot, with many a cruel hete
  Gan Troilus upon his helm to-bete " (V.
    1758–1762),

are too indefinite in their statements to
specify whether one or more authorities are
referred to.

Again, he does not care to give on his own
authority statements which he has not found
vouched for elsewhere : —

" But whether that she children hadde or
    noon,
  I rede it nought; therefore I lete it goon "
    (I. 132–133).

" But how it was, certayn, can I not seye,
  If that his lady understood not this,
  Or feyned hir she niste, oon of the tweye ;
  But wel I rede that, by no maner weye,
  Ne semed it as that she of him roughte,
  Nor of his peyne, or what-so-ever he thoughte "
    (I. 492–497).

unless it may be upon a matter of his own experience : —

" But as we may alday our-selven see,
  Through more wode or col, the more fyr;
  Right so encrees of hope, of what it be,
  Therwith ful ofte encreseth eek desyr;
  Or, as an ook cometh of a litel spyr,
  So through this lettre, which that she him sente,
  Encresen gan desyr, of which he brente.
  Wherfore I seye alwey, that day and night
  This Troilus gan to desiren more
  Than he dide erst, thurgh hope " [1] (II. 1331–
      1340).

He makes a point of referring his readers who are interested in the fate of Troy to the books devoted to that subject : —

" But how this toun com to destruccioun
  Ne falleth nough to purpos me to telle ;

---

[1] As illustrative of Chaucer's process of composition it may be noted that II. 1331–1337 are not based upon the corresponding stanza in the *Filostrato* (III. 130); the comparison II. 1335 is taken from the *Liber Parabolorum* of Alain de Lille (Migne, *Patrologia*, vol. CCX. col.

For it were here a long disgressioun
Fro my matere, and for yow long to dwelle.
But the Troyane gestes, as they felle,
In Omer, or in Dares, or in *Dyte*,
Who-so that can, may rede hem as they
    wryte " (I. 141–147).

and, as the theme of his poem is the love
of Troilus for Criseyde, those who wish to
know of his warlike exploits must go elsewhere for information : —

" And if I hadde y-taken for to wryte
The armes of this ilke worthy man,
Than wolde I of his batailles endyte.
But for that I to wryte first began
Of his love, I have seyd as that I can.
His worthy dedes, who-so list hem here,
Reed Dares, he can tell hem alle y-fere (V.
    1765–1771).

Lydgate, in the " Prologue " to his
Tragedies, a free paraphrase in verse of

583 ; cf. E. Koeppel, *Herrig's Archiv*, vol. XC. p. 150),
while the conclusion II. 1338–1340 is a translation of the
mere statement of fact by Boccaccio. (*Fil.*, III. 131, 1–3;
cf. 130, 7.)

the French prose version by Laurent de Premierfait of Boccaccio's *De Casibus Virorum*[1] in his "list" of Chaucer's works, notes that: —

"In youthe he made a translation
Of a boke which called is Trophe
In Lumbard tonge as men may rede and se
And in our vulgare, long or that he dyed
Gave it to name of Troylus and Creseyde."[2]

---

[1] T. Warton, *History of English Poetry*, ed. 1840, vol. II. pp. 277–278, 320. P. Paris, *Les manuscripts françois de la Bibliotheque du Roi*, Paris, 1836–1848, vol. I. pp. 233–260; II. 231–244; V. 119–122. A. Hortis, *Studi sulle opere latine del Boccaccio*, Trieste, 1879, pp. 638–642. E. Koeppel, *Laurents und Lydgates Bearbeitungen von Boccaccio's Casibus Virorum*, Munich, 1885.

[2] *The Tragedies gathered by Jhon Bochas of all such Princes as fell from theyr estates throughe the mutability of Fortune since the Creacion of Adam until his time ; wherein may be seen what vices bring mene to destruccion, with notable warninges howe the like may be avoydde. Translated into English by John Lidgate, Monke of Burye*, edition of J. Wayland, 1558; cf. T. F. Dibdin, *Typographical Antiquities*, 1816, vol. III. pp. 530–531. This seems to be the "undated black-letter edition" cited by Skeat. *Minor Poems of Chaucer*, p. x.

Again, in his version of the *Historia Trojana* of Guido delle Colonne, in the translation of the critical discussion of the writers upon the Trojan war, Homer, Virgil, Ovid, Dictys, and Dares, such as he found it in his original,[1] depending, doubtless, upon the list in Chaucer's *Hous of Fame*, he adds without comment a new name, —

---

[1] Warton was uncertain whether Lydgate's *Troy-book* was a direct translation from the work of Guido, or from a French version of the Latin original. (*Hist. of Eng. Poetry*, 1840, vol. II. p. 292.) A. Joly thought that the Latin original had been amplified by the use of Benoit's poem. (*Benoît de Ste. More et le Roman de Troie ou les métamorphoses d'Homère et de l'épopée gréco-latine au moyen-âge*, vol. II. pp. 494–496.) Henry Bradshaw regarded the Latin work as the original of this, as well as the other English versions. (*Proceedings of the Cambridge Antiquarian Soc.*, vol. III.) Sidney Lee, evidently upon the sole authority of the title-page, stated that "Lydgate mainly paraphrased ' Guido di Colonne's *Historia de Bello Trojano* ' and perhaps Dares Phrygius and Dictys Cretensis." (*Dict. of Nat. Biog.*, vol. XXXIV. p. 312.) Schick seems to think that a French source was used in conjunction with the Latin work. (*Lydgate's Temple of Glass*, p. cxvii.; cf. *Troy-book*, sig. b 2 verso, col. 1.)

"And of this syege wrote eke Lollius."[1]

And when he comes to the episode of Troilus and Criseyde in his original, he states
that he will not give it in full : —

> "Syth my maister Chaucer here afore
> In this matter hath so well him bore,
> In his boke of Troylus and Creseyde
> Which he mayde longe or that he deyde."[2]

In the first edition of the works of
Chaucer which contained anything in the
way of a commentary,[3] that of Speght,

[1] *The Auncient Historie and onely Trewe and sincere
Cronicle of the Warres betwixte the Grecians and Troyanes.
. . . Wrytten by Daretus a Troyan, and Dictus a Grecian
. . . and Digested in Latyn by the lerned Guydo de Columpnis and sythes translated by John Lidgate Moncke of Burye.*
Thomas Marshe, 1555, sig. b 2 verso, col. 1.   Cf. Dibdin,
l.c., vol. IV. pp. 494–496.   I cite this as *Troy-book*.

[2] *l.c.*, sig. R 2 verso, col. 1.

[3] The *Troilus* had already been printed in the "Works
of Chaucer," in the editions of Pynson, 1526; of W.
Thynne, 1532 and 1542; and the reprints of the latter
in 1550 and 1561; as well as separately by Caxton, *ab.*
1483; Wynkyn de Worde, 1517; Pynson, 1526. (Henry
Bradshaw, *ap. Francis Thynne's Animadversions*, ed. F. J.

published in 1598, in the section of the
introduction which treats of the works of
the poet, the editor writes: —

"Troilus and Creseid called Throphee in
the Lumbard tongue, translated not verbatim,
but the argument thence taken, and most
cunningly amplified by Chaucer."[1]

This magisterial sentence seems to imply
that Speght had information of a definite
nature upon the sources of the *Troilus*
other than that given in Lydgate's lines;
but his restatement of the same matter in
the corresponding passage, in his edition
of 1602, promptly disposes of such a suggestion.

"Troilus and Creseid called Throphe in the
Lumbard tongue was translated out of Latin, as
in the Preface to the Seconde booke of Troilus
and Creseid he confesseth in these words, —

Furnivall, 1875, p. 70 n.   Cf. Skeat in *Works of Chaucer*,
vol. II. pp. lxxv–lxxvi.)

[1] *Workes of Chaucer*, 1598, sig. c 1 recto.

'To every lover I me excuse,
That of no sentement I this endite,
But out of Latin in my tonge it write.' "[1]

His identification of Lollius as " an Italian Historiographer borne in the citie of Urbine " in his list of *Most of the Authors cited by G. Chaucer in his works by name declared*,[2] has the merit of being specific as to the author, if not supplying information about his work and the language in which it was written.

[1] *Workes of Chaucer*, 1602, sig. c 1 recto.

[2] Cf. *Francis Thynne's Animadversions*, p. 71. " The fourthe thinge ys, that in the catalogue of the auctours, you have omytted manye auctours vouched by Chaucer; and therefore dyd rightlye intitle yt, 'most,' and not all, of the auctours cited by geffrye Chawcer." In the edition of 1602, Speght obviated this criticism by writing, " The authors cited by G. Chaucer in his workes by name declared." Dryden's information about the source of Chaucer's *Troilus* is due to Speght (*Works of Dryden*, ed. Scott-Saintsbury, vol. VI. p. 225), to whom he is indebted in other ways. Cf. F. H. Tupper, *Mod. Lang. Notes*, vol. XII. pp. 347–352; cf. Douce, *Illustrations of Shakespeare* (1807), p. 64.

ç

Sir Henry Savile, in his edition of the work *De Causa Dei contra Pelagas* of Bishop Thomas Bradwardine (1290(?)–1349), published in 1618, suggested that the discourse upon predestination in the *Troilus* (IV. 966–1078) and in the *Nonne Preestes Tale*,[1] where the author's name is mentioned, bespoke an acquaintance with his work.[2]

Sir Francis Kinaston, who in 1635 published the first two books of his Latin version of the *Troilus*, in which the metrical structure of the original was preserved in

---

[1] *C. T.*, Group B, 4432.

[2] Life of Chaucer in *Preface* to Urry's edition of 1721; also quotation in *Testimonies* of same edition. Speght gives as the Argument of the poem, "In which discourse Chaucer liberally treateth of the divine purveiaunce." (*Workes of Chaucer*, 1598; sig. c 5 verso; ed. 1602; sig. Bb 5 recto.) The author of the *Testament of Love* had already referred to the same passage as authoritative on the matter. (Book III. ch. IV. 248 ff. in W. W. Skeat, *Chaucerian and Other Pieces*, p. 123.) Cf. Lounsbury, *Studies in Chaucer*, vol. I. pp. 202–204.

the number of lines to a stanza, of sylla-
bles to the line, and in the order of the
rimes,[1] in his English commentary on the
poem, noting the great difference between
the story of certain characters in the Trojan legend, as found in Chaucer's poem,
and that in other sources, writes : —

"Some do not improbably conjecture that
Chaucer, in writing the loves and lives of Troilus and Creseid, did rather glance at some pri-
vate persons, as one of king *Edward* the third's
sons, and a lady of the court, his paramour;
then [than] follow *Homer, Dares Phyrius*, or
any author writing the history of those times;
for first, it cannot be imagined that *Chaucer*,
being soe great a learned scholler, could be
ignorant of the story; next that he should soe
mistake as to make Creseid the daughter of
Calchus, the soothsayer, who was the daughter
of one Chryses, and there uppon called Chry-
seis, whereas her right name was Astynome;
then there should be any love between Troilus

---

[1] *Amorum Troili et Creseidæ*, Libri duo priores,
Oxoniæ, 1635; cf. Lounsbury, *l.c.*, vol. III. pp. 77–78.

and her; especially that Chaucer should personate her as a widdow, whereas she was a votary to Diana."[1]

Timothy Thomas, in his preface to Urry's edition of Chaucer, published in 1721, has little to add concerning the sources of the *Troilus;* he repeats Speght's statements about "Lollius" and "Trophe" and then goes on to say:—

"He has not contented himself with a bare translation of his Author, but hath added several things of his own, and borrowed from

---

[1] *The Loves of Troilus and Creseid*, written by Chaucer; with a commentary, by Sir Francis Kinaston, never before published. London. Printed for and sold by F. G. Waldron, MDCCXVI. pp. 7–8; (first part) cf. Lounsbury, *l.c.*, vol. III. pp. 81–82. Urry, in preparing his edition of Chaucer, had drawn notes from the apparently unique manuscript of Kinaston's complete work, and these were used by Thomas. Cf. *Preface* to Urry's *Chaucer*, sig. m; *Glossary*, p. 47. *The Loves*, etc., pp. i.–ii., vii., xi.–xii. After Waldron's death, we find the manuscript in possession of W. S. Singer. Cf. *Works of Chaucer*. Cheswick, 1822, vol. I. pp. xx.–xxi., n.; *Notes and Queries*, I. 5, 252.

others what he thought proper for the Embellishment of this work, and particularly the song of Troilus in the First Book is a Translation of that song in Petrarch which begins, S' amor non e, Che dunqu' e quel ch' io sento?"

and he then refers to the comments of Savile and Kinaston, which have been mentioned above, and in the *Glossary* under Lollius, he writes:—

" An Italian Historiographer born at Urbino, who lived under the Emperors Macrinus and Heliogabalus, in the beginning of the Third Century, is said to have written the *History of His Own Time*, and also the *Life of the Emperor Diadumenus, the Son of Macrinus.*" [1]

It was Thomas Tyrwhitt, to whom students of Chaucer owe the most for the elucidation of the poet's work, particularly of the *Canterbury Tales*, who was the first

[1] Tyrwhitt showed clearly that Thomas was the editor of the 1721 Chaucer, after the death of Urry. *The Poetical Works of Geoffrey Chaucer.* Ed. T. Tyrwhitt. London, 1855, p. vii. and note *n*.

to point out the immediate source of the story of the poem. In his *Essay on the Language and Versification of Chaucer*, prefaced to his edition of the *Canterbury Tales*, he stated that in his opinion "Chaucer was to the full as much obliged to Boccacce in his *Troilus* as in his *Knight's Tale*."[1] In his notes and glossary he shows that he has made a careful comparison of the English poem with the Italian original,[2] points out the indebtedness to the *De Consolatione Philosophiæ* of Boethius in the passage treating of predestination,[3] notices that the sonnet of Petrarch was translated as the work of Lollius,[4] whose identity he leaves as a puzzle,[5] and would identify Chaucer's own mention of Trophe,

"At bothe the worldes endes saith Trophee
In stede of boundes he a pillar set,"[6]

[1] *Poetical Works of G. Chaucer*, p. xxxix. note 62.
[2] *Ibid.*, pp. 182, 190, 205, 209, 457, 471, 476, 483, 486, 495.
[3] *Ibid.*, p. 457.   [4] *Ibid.*, pp. 209, 483.   [5] *Ibid.*, pp. 209, 479.
[6] *C. T.*, 14123–14124.   Ed. Tyrwhitt.

and Lydgate's Trophe, with the *Filostrato*.[1]
He also suggests that the "Latin" from
which language Chaucer stated he had
translated his poem was Italian, as Boccaccio in the *Teseide*[2] — to which the English poet was under obligations in his
Parlement of Foules,[3] *Anelida and Arcite*,[4]

[1] *Poetical Works of Chaucer*, pp. 203, 209, 495.

[2] *Teseide*, II. 2, 4. Cf. *Poetical Works*, etc., p. liv. n.

[3] *Poetical Works*, etc., p. 179; cf. ten Brink, *Chaucer. Studien zur Geschichte seiner Entwickelung*, pp. 125–
128.

[4] ten Brink, *l.c.*, pp. 49–53, 56. On *Palamon and
Arcite*, Chaucer's early translation of the *Teseide*, which,
it has been conjectured, was written in seven-verse
stanzas, and utilized in some of his latter works; cf. ten
Brink, *l.c.*, pp. 39–70; J. Koch, *Eng. Stud.*, I. pp. 249 ff.;
XXVII. pp. 3, 12; A. W. Pollard, *Globe Chaucer*, pp. xxvi.–
xxvii.; F. J. Mather, *An English Miscellany Presented to
Dr. Furnivall*, pp. 301 ff. Tyrwhitt, who suggested that
Palamon and Arcite was a translation of the *Teseida* (*l.c.*,
p. xxxix. and note 62, liii.), did not note the parallel
passages in *Anelida and Arcite*, and supposed that the
later poem was written before Chaucer's acquaintance
with Boccaccio's work (*l.c.*, p. 445), and W. Hertzberg
adopted this view (*Chaucer's Canterbury-geschichten*, 1866,
pp. 61, 595), which was successfully combated by ten

Troilus[1] and the *Knight's Tale*[2] — had referred to his own language as "Latino
volgare." [3]

Warton, in his *History of English Poetry*,
quotes Lydgate's statement concerning the
source of the poem, which he thinks is in
conflict with what Chaucer himself says
about the language of the work he is translating, speaks of the conjecture of Speght,
whose name he does not mention, upon
"Lollius," refers to the historian of the
third century, Lollius Urbicus, none of
whose works are extant, although Du
Cange puts him in his list of authorities
in his *Glossarium*, who, however, "could
not be Chaucer's Lollius," who in the

Brink (*l.c.*, pp. 49, 53–56), whose theory on this point is
accepted by Mather (*l.c.*, pp. 307–312).

[1] *Poet. Works*, p. 182.

[2] *Thynnes Animadversions*, ed. Furnivall, p. 43; *Poet.
Works*, pp. liii.–lvi., 178–182; T. Warton, *Hist. of Eng.
Poetry*, 1774, vol. I. pp. 344, 357.

[3] *Poet. Works*, p. 209. A view accepted by Skeat.
Works of Chaucer, vol. II. p. 468.

Hous of Fame is placed amongst the historians of Troy, and calls attention to the fact that the names Monesteo, Rupheo, and Phebuseo[1] denoted an Italian original. He points out a number of the passages[2] in the *Troilus* in which Chaucer comments upon the closeness with which he follows his authority; and mentions the indebtedness of the English poem to Boethius, Petrarch, and Bradwardine — the last as if assured as the others.[3]

At a later date, from information received from Tyrwhitt,[4] he knew that the *Filostrato* was the direct source of the larger part of the English poem,[5] whereas before, knowing merely the title of Boc-

---

[1] *T. and C.*, II. 51–54.

[2] *T. and C.*, II. 10; III. 576, 1330, 1823.

[3] T. Warton, *l.c.*, vol. I. pp. 384–388.

[4] On Warton's great indebtedness to Tyrwhitt, cf. Ritson, *Observations on the First Three Volumes of the History of English Poetry*, 1782, pp. 30, 31, 33, 48. On Warton's ignorance of Italian, *ibid.*, pp. 30, 38.

[5] *Hist. of Eng. Poetry*, 1840, vol. II. p. 162, note.

caccio's work, he had thought that it only treated of the same subject.[1]

William Godwin, in his *Life of Chaucer*, published in 1803, which "may, indeed, be declared to deserve the distinction of being the most worthless piece of biography in the English language,"[2] disputes Tyrwhitt's view in every particular. He asserts that without question the *Troilus* is a translation of the Latin work *Trophe* of Lollius, not the Lollius Urbicus of the third century, but a contemporary of Wace and Thomas of Becket,[3] the author, also, of the original of the story of *Palamon and Arcite*.[4] He asks whether it is probable that Chaucer would consult a less known work of Boccaccio, when in the *Clerk's Tale* he does not show an

[1] *Hist. of Eng. Poetry*, 1778, vol. I, p. 385; II. p. 25.

[2] Lounsbury, *l.c.*, vol. I. p. 194.

[3] W. Godwin, *Life of Chaucer*, 1804, vol. I. pp. 419, 429–430, 437–438.

[4] *l.c.*, vol. III. p. 17, note.

acquaintance with the *Decameron*, the work by which the author is generally known.[1]

W. W. Singer, in the introduction to the poems of Chaucer, published in 1822 in the Chiswick collection of English poets, shows that he had made a careful comparison of the English and Italian poems, stating that the *Troilus* was " for the most part a translation of the *Filostrato* of Boccaccio, but with many variations and large additions, amounting to no less than 2700 verses." Chaucer's references to " Lollius " and to " Latin " were surprising, " for nothing can be more certain than that Boccaccio was his original; the fable and characters are the

[1] *l.c.*, vol. II. p. 473. Sir Walter Scott, whose review of Godwin's book in the *Edinburgh Review*, can only find its equal for severity in Lowell's criticism on Masson's *Milton*, on this point rejected Tyrwhitt's opinion in favor of Godwin's. (*Works of Dryden*, ed. Scott-Saintsbury, vol. VI. p. 243.)

same in both poems, and numerous passages of the *Filostrato* are literally translated."[1]

After such a clear statement of the case as this, it was certainly "far ritroso calle," when, twenty years later, G. L. Craik in his *Sketches of the History of Literature and Learning in England from the Norman Conquest to the Accession of Elizabeth,* not only refused to credit the *Filostrato* as being the source of the *Troilus,* but asserted that Chaucer was quite ignorant of the Italian language,[2] a position in conflict with the undisputed statements of Lydgate and W. Thynne.[3] Again Sir Harris Nicolas, in his *Life of Chaucer,* prefixed to the Aldine edition of

---

[1] *The Poems of G. Chaucer,* Chiswick, 1822, vol. I. p. xix.; cf. p. xvi.

[2] *Sketches, etc.,* 1844, vol. II. pp. 47–53. Again in his *History of English Literature,* 1861, vol. I. pp. 272–276.

[3] With Lydgate's statement concerning the source of the *Troilus* may be compared his problematical lines con-

Chaucer, in 1845, took the same position, remarking that those who thought differently were but "indiscriminate worshippers of genius who endow their idols with all human attainments." [1]

cerning a translation made by Chaucer, *Tragedies*, etc., sig. a 2 verso, col. 1.

> "He wrote also full many a day agone
> Dant in English, himselfe so doth expresse."

On interpretation of his passage, cf. W. W. Skeat's totally wrong one, *Chaucer's Minor Poems*, pp. xi–xii.; 2d ed., p. 477. E. Koeppel, *Laurent Premierfaits und J. Lydgates Bearbeitungen*, etc., p. 82. *Anglia*, vol. XIII. p. 186. Lounsbury, *l.c.*, vol. II. p. 425. Depending upon this statement, Speght in his 1598 *Chaucer* gives in the list of the poet's works, *Dantem Italum transtulit* followed by the statement, *Petrarchæ quædam transtulit*, (sig. c 1 recto), but both these statements are omitted in the 1602 edition. Thynne, who, as has been noticed (p. 24, n. 2), was the first to point out the source of the *Knight's Tale*, has elsewhere the statement, "unleste a manne be a good saxoniste, frenche and Italyane linguiste (from whence Chaucer has borrowed manye words)." *Animadversions*, p. 31; cf. p. 43. Against Craik's opinion, cf. Fiedler, *Herrigs Archiv*, vol. II. p. 151; Kissner, *Chaucer*, etc., p. 6; ten Brink, *Chaucer*, p. 186.

[1] *Works of Chaucer* . . . 1845, vol. I. p. 25; Yet he quotes Lydgate's statement on the matter (p. 100.),

In his edition of Chaucer published
1854–1856, R. Bell showed that he could
believe the evidence of his own eyes. In
his *Memoir of Chaucer* he notices that
no such author "called Lollius," or book
"called Trophe," had ever been discovered, accepting the opinion of Tyrwhitt
upon the first point to the prejudice of
that of Godwin.[1]   He did not consider
seriously Nicolas's opinion upon Chaucer's
knowledge of Italian; besides making the
general statement that " the substance of
the poem, which Chaucer amplified and
altered, is to be found in the *Filostrato*
of Boccaccio," [2] in the *Introduction* to the

and Tyrwhitt's remarks on the source of the *Troilus*, in
his *Essay on the Language and Versification of Chaucer*,
which is reprinted in this edition, is found later on (*l.c.*,
pp. 225–226, n.).   This note is omitted in Morris's edition of 1866, where Skeat's treatment of the versification
is substituted for that of Tyrwhitt (vol. I. p. 172).

[1] *Poetical Works of Geoffrey Chaucer*, edited by Rob-
ert Bell, vol. I. p. 14; cf. vol. III. p. 10.

[2] *l.c.*, vol. I. p. 14.

Troilus, the general features of the two poems are compared and at the same time examples of Chaucer's mode of translation are noted, while parallel passages from the Italian poem are cited in notes to the text.[1] It is noted that the earliest source of the story was "a prose chronicle . . . by Guido de Colonna," which must have been drawn "from some metrical romance extant in his time," and the fact that Chaucer elsewhere mentions Guido denoted that he was acquainted with him "either through his works or reputation." Lydgate's "Trophe" is explained as "a name denoting Troylus's change of fortune."[2]

It was by others than English editors

[1] *l.c.*, vol. V. pp. 10–14, 17–254; VI. pp. 5–52.

[2] *l.c.*, vol. V. pp. 9–10. The collaboration of Rev. J. M. Jephson in this edition may be noted. The information of the editors about Lollius Urbicus, the *Roman de Troilus*, — which they regard as the original of Guido, when, in fact, it is a translation of Boccaccio's poem, —

of Chaucer that the next step forward
was made, in the study of the sources of
the *Troilus*. In 1858 L. Moland and C.
D'Héricault, in the Introduction to their
edition of *Nouvelles Françoises en prose
du XIVe siecle*, in giving a detailed account of the literary history of Troilus,
were the first to point out that the *Filostrato* had its antecedents in the *Roman
de Troie* of Benoit de Sainte-More,[1] and
Guido delle Colonne's[2] *Historia Trojana*,[3]
and had no doubt that the English poem
was in the main an imitation of the Italian
poem.[4] To explain the name Lollius they
suggested that as the late fourteenth-cen-
tury French romance *Le Livre de Troilus*

and the *Historia Trojana*, as an authority on the siege
of Thebes, is taken from Warton without acknowledg-
ment. Cf. E. Koeppel, *Lydgate's Story of Thebes*, p. 17.

[1] "Benoit de Saint Maur," as they write it (*Nouvelles François*, pp. lix, lx.).

[2] "Guido delle Columne," "Guy des Colonnes," (*l.c.*,
p. lxxx.).   [3] *l.c.*, pp. lix.–xciii.   [4] *l.c.*, xci.–xcviii.

was stated by its author to be a translation of the *Filostrato* " composé par un poethe florentin nommé Petrarque," [1] Chaucer, not knowing the name of the author of his original, adopted that of Lollius.[2] Their suggestion, which was only hazarded in a note, concerning Lydgate's *Trophe*, can only be given in their own words: "Indiquons que *trophe* représente assez bien le vieux mot trufe, truphe (bourde, tromperie), italianisé. Chaucer a-t-il *truphé* Lydgate ou Lydgate le public." [3]

Sandras was the first to suggest that the work of Benoit might be the direct source of certain passages in the *Troilus*, in his *Étude sur Chaucer consideré comme imitateur des trouvères*, published in 1859, printing a number of passages from the unedited *Roman de Troie* to substantiate

---

[1] *l.c.*, pp. ci, 120.   [2] *l.c.*, xcviii.–c.

[3] *l.c.*, p. c., n.   They were not acquainted with Chaucer's own mention of " Trophe."

D

his conjecture, but his parallel citations are neither definite nor full enough to be conclusive. He, too, thinks that Boccaccio is hidden under the name of Lollius.[1]

In 1862 A. Ebert, in his brief recension of the work of Sandras, expressed the opinion that while there was reason to justify the assumption that Chaucer had recourse to other works than the *Filostrato*, there was not evidence enough to show whether it was to the work of Benoit or to that of Guido — which he regarded as an original production — he was indebted for the introduction of episodes, not found in the Italian poem.[2]

In 1867 Kissner clearly showed by the citation of parallel passages that the English poem was in large part a translation

---

[1] *Étude*, etc., pp. 42–50, 263–283; cf. Hertzberg, *Jahr. der deutschen Shakespeare-Gesellschaft*, vol. VI. p. 202.

[2] *Jahr. f. rom. u. engl. Lit.*, vol. IV. pp. 89–91.

of Boccaccio's work, in which the order of the stanzas, the verses, and even the rime of the original were adhered to as closely as possible,[1] took the same position as Ebert in regard to Chaucer's other sources for the story, considering Guido, however, as a plagiarist.[2] He believed that by Lollius, Boccaccio was intended, — a deliberate expedient used elsewhere by the English poet to mystify his readers.[3] "Trophe," mentioned by Chaucer in the *Monkes Tale*, he supposed referred to the *De Casibus Virorum* of Boccaccio.[4]

In the same year Henry Morley, in his

[1] A. Kissner, *Chaucer in seinen Beziehungen zur italienischen Literature*, Bonn, 1867, pp. 12–22, 25–58.

[2] *l.c.*, pp. 22–25.

[3] *l.c.*, pp. 7–9. Cf. Hertzberg, *Chaucers Canterburygeschichten*, 1866, pp. 42, 44; *Jahr. f. rom. u. engl. Lit.*, vol. VIII. pp. 154–155. Henry Bradshaw independently reached the same conclusion, G. W. Prothero, *Memoir of H. Bradshaw*, p. 216. For a conflicting view, cf. Lounsbury, *l.c.*, vol. II. p. 413.

[4] Kissner, *l.c.*, p. 8.

English Writers, gave a comparative analysis of the two poems, noting that Chaucer's version " was more than half as long again as its original," [1] and proved to his own satisfaction that " Latin " was Italian,[2] that the English poet, in " his labour towards the elevation of the *Filostrato*," [3] " with a parable of Scripture in his mind, out of Lolium, the Latin for a tare, probably contrived for Boccaccio a name that he thought justly significant," [4] and that Lydgate referred to the *Filostrato* as " Trophe," because " it evidently points to Criseyde's perfidy, and is related to $\tau\rho o\pi\grave{\eta}$, a turning." [5]   He also noted that the additions to the narrative concerning

[1] *English Writers*, 1867, vol. II. Part I. pp. 237–243. To give preciseness to his comparison, without regard to the amount utilized by the English poet, he states that the *Filostrato* contains 5352 lines, and the *Troilus*, 8251. Cf. Rossetti, *Comparison*, etc., p. iii.; Skeat, *Works of Chaucer*, 1894, vol. II. pp. xlix–l.

[2] *l.c.*, p. 243.   [3] *l.c.*, p. 244, n.   [4] *l.c.*, p. 243.
[5] *l.c.*, p. 221, n.

the actions of the heroine in the Greek camp, and her dialogue with Diomedes and with her father,[1] show that Chaucer was acquainted with either the work of Benoit or the Latin version of Guido.[2]

In a communication to the *Athenæum* for Sept. 26, 1868, are set forth the views of W. M. Rossetti, who regarded Lydgate's " Trophe " as the English " trophy," a trophy or victim of love, which corresponds to Boccaccio's own definition of the title of the *Filostrato ;* and hence the term " Trophe " is applied to that work by Lydgate. Chaucer, as the French translator, considered Petrarch its author, and referred to him as Lollius in the *Troilus* and the *Hous of Fame,* — though he introduces him with his real name in the *Clerkes Tale* — because one of his correspondents ad-

---

[1] This is one of the points wrongly made by Sandras and rectified by Hertzberg, *Jahrbuch der Shakespeare-Gesellschaft,* vol. VI. p. 202.   [2] *l.c.,* p. 243.

dressed him as Laelius.[1]   This communication led Latham, in the next number of
the same journal, to offer his most ingen-
ious explanation of Lollius.   He suggested
that Chaucer got the idea that Lollius was
a writer on the Trojan war by the misinterpretation prevalent in Chaucer's time
of the opening lines of one of the Epistles
of Horace,

" Trojani belli scriptorem, maxime Lolli
  Dum tu declamas Romæ, Præneste relegi "
    (Ep. I, 2),

which gave the idea that " the name of
the person addressed had become attached
to the person written about." [2]

---

[1] Rossetti, in his *Chaucer's Troylus and Cryseyde
compared with Boccaccio's Filostrato*, 1873, pp. vii.–viii.,
gives up his explanation of Lollius in favor of that of
Latham, but still credits his own explanation of Trophe.

[2] *Athenæum*, Oct. 3, 1868, p. 433.   Rossetti, *Comparison*, etc., p. vii., writes that this suggestion was " made
or rather repeated " in the place cited; but I am not
acquainted with its earlier mention.

Hertzberg, in his review of Kissner's book, accepted his thesis in full,[1] and to obviate the difficulty of the "Trophe" question suggested that the line on the *Monkes Tale*

" At both the worldes endes, saith Trophe "

should be read,

" At both the Worldes endes, as Trophe,"

even though the false reading was as old as Lydgate's time.[2]

Ten Brink, in his literary study of Chaucer, accepted Tyrwhitt's suggestion that by "Latin" Italian was meant, Rossetti's explanation of Lydgate's "Trophe" and Hertzberg's correction of the Chaucerian text,[3] and in confirmation of Latham's conjecture about "Lollius" — a

---

[1] *Jahr. f. rom. u. engl. Lit.*, vol. VIII. (1866), pp. 156–162.   [2] *l.c.*, p. 155.

[3] *Chaucer, Studien zur Geschichte seiner Entwickelung*, pp. 68–70, 182–184.

conclusion he had arrived at independently — suggested that it was not due to a current misinterpretation, but that in the manuscript of Horace used by Chaucer, the incorrect readings *scriptorum* and *te legi* substituted for *scriptorem* and *relegi*.[1] He also noticed that details in the *Troilus* were due to the work of either Be-

---

[1] *l.c.*, pp. 85–87. Skeat, *Works of Chaucer*, ed. 1878, vol. I., p. 18, n. *Chaucer, The Minor Poems*, 1888, p. 359, *Works of Chaucer*, 1894 (vol. III. p. 278), and Rossetti (*l.c.*, p. 359). *Works of Chaucer*, 1894 (vol. III. p. 278) and Rossetti (*l.c.*, p. vii.) accept Latham's suggestion as almost a certainty. Joly (*Benoît de Ste. Maure*, etc., vol. I. pp. 216–217), and Hertzberg (*Shakespeare Jahr.* vol. VI., p. 201, n. 2) concur in general statement of both Latham and ten Brink, without expressing their precise position in regard to secondary matters. Yet Lounsbury (*l.c.*, vol. II. p. 410) states that "By no stretch of language can [it] be regarded as probable." Yet the main premise for this opinion — to wit, that when Chaucer could translate a philosophical work, the *De Consolatione* of Boethius, he would not have made the slip of mistaking a genitive for an ablative — is somewhat vitiated, when we consider that a French translation of the Latin work was Chaucer's original. Cf. Rossetti, *Comparison*, p. vii., n.; M. H. Liddell, *Globe Chaucer*, p. xl.

noit or Guido or of both, but the suggestion is confessedly not his own.[1]

In 1869–1870, by the quite independent investigations of Dunger and Joly,
the impudent plagiarisim of the *Roman
de Troie* by Guido delle Colonne was put
beyond a doubt by extensive comparisons
of the French and Latin works;[2] but

[1] *l.c.*, p. 85.

[2] A. Joly, *Benoît de Ste. Maure et le Roman de Troie*,
1870–1871, vol. II. 470–484. H. Dunger, *Die Sage vom
trojanischen Kriege in den Bearbeitungen des Mittelalters
und ihren antiken Quellen*, Leipzig, 1869, pp. 39, 61–64.
Tyrwhitt was acquainted with both works, and suspected
that the *Roman de Troie* was the direct source of Guido's
work, but "a full discussion of the point by a comparison
of Guido's work with the Roman de Troye, would require
more time and pains than I am inclined to bestow on it"
(note to *C. T.*, 15147, *Works of Chaucer*, p. 204. Cf.
note to *C. T.*, 14914, p. 204, pp. 471, 486). Warton in his
first volume of his *History of English Poetry* (1774) only
mentioned Guido as the author of an original work upon
the Troy legend, for the sources of which he accepts the
author's own statements, and "from which Chaucer de-
rived his ideas about the Trojan story" (vol. I. (1774),
pp. 126–127; cf. pp. 138, 385, vol. II. pp. 82–83, 91–92, 97,
on acquaintance with Guido's work; cf. E. Koeppel, *Lyd-*

these two scholars in their orientations of the whole mediæval Troy legend, only touched incidentally upon the matter of the original of Chaucer's *Troilus*, and failed to notice the secondary sources

gate's *Story of Thebes*, pp. 16–17), and knew of Benoit's work and its subject at only second hand (vol. I. p. 136). In a note in the second volume, from information unquestionably received from Tyrwhitt, he speaks of "the ancient metrical one of Benoit, to whom, I believe, Colonna is much indebted" (vol. II. (1778) p. 99, n.). Francis Douce, in his *Illustrations of Shakespeare*, published in 1807, stated that he had made the comparison suggested by Tyrwhitt, and found that Guido had "only translated the Norman writer into Latin" (vol. II. pp. 65–66), but his correct conclusion, even if the detailed results were not published, did not seem to be generally known, even though it found its way into such a popular work as Dunlop's *History of Fiction* (pp. 175–176, ed. 1845). In 1857 Fromman expressed the opinion that Guido's work was nothing but a translation of the French poem (*Germania*, vol. II. p. 52), while in 1858 Moland and d'Héricault (*l.c.*, p. lxxx.) regarded the Latin work as "une amplification de l'ouvrage de Daurès — mais aux merites de laquelle Benoit de Saint-Maur n'a pas per contribué." Pey in the next year (*Jahr. f. rom. und engl. Lit.*, I. 228) fostered the theory that both Guido and Benoit based their works upon an original unabridged text of Dares, which has not

which contributed to the story of the
English poem.[1] Joly, to be sure, mentioned Latham's and ten Brink's suggestion as if it were his own, and proposed
that Lydgate's line,

"Of a boke whiche called is Trophe,"

if restored to its probably true reading,
which could so easily have been corrupted,

"Of a boke whiche called is Strophe,"

come down to us. This view was accepted by Ebert (*l.c.*,
vol. IV. p. 90) and Cholevius (*Geschichte der deutschen
Poesie*, vol. I. pp. 111–112) ; but regarded with doubt by
Kissner (*l.c.*, p. 23, n.), and one would have thought
finally disposed of by Hertzberg (*l.c.*, pp. 187–194), who
like Barth (*Guido de Columna*, p. 19) and Morf (*Rom.*,
vol. XXI. pp. 18–21) denied Guido even an acquaintance
with the Dares as we have it; if Koerting (*Dictys and
Dares*, 1874, pp. 67, 95 ; *Boccaccio*, 1881, pp. 586–587) and
Greif (*Die mittelalterlichen Bearbeitungen der Trojanersage*,
p. 62) had not adopted it as a thesis the maintenance of
which was all important, and if Constans (*Hist. de la lit-
terature et langue française*, vol. I. p. 215, n. 1) did not
seem half inclined to accept their conclusions.

[1] Joly, *l.c.*, p. 515; Dunger, *l.c.*, p. 36.

would refer to the Italian poem, thus denoted on account of its metrical structure.[1]

W. Hertzberg in a study upon the *Troilus* legend independently reached the same general conclusions, and, in commenting upon Kissner's results, noted that while only two-thirds of the 5288 lines of the *Filostrato* had been used in the *Troilus,* that the English poem contained 8251 lines. He further pointed out three passages in the *Troilus* which might equally as well have come from either the work of Benoit or Guido, and three others which from the similarity of language could only have had their sources in the French poem.[2]

F. Mamroth in his work, *G. Chaucer, seine zeit und Seine Abhaengigkeit von Boc-*

---

[1] Joly, *l.c.,* p. 216–217, 493.

[2] *Jahr. der deutschen Shakespeare-Gesellschaft,* vol. VI. (1871), pp. 201–205. I refer to this article as Hertzberg, *l.c.*

caccio, although not doubting the Italian source of the *Troilus*, upon the authority of Bell and Hertzberg, still thought Godwin's view worthy of an analysis.[1]

W. M. Rossetti said the final word upon the *Filostrato-Troilus* question by the publication in 1873 of his line-for-line comparison of the two poems, showing that somewhat less than a third of the English poem· was taken directly from the *Filostrato*.[2] Although he gives an analysis of the *Troilus* story in the *Roman de Troie* for the sake of setting it off against that given in the Italian poem, he nowhere suggests that Chaucer adopted hints from the French poet, or his Latin plagiarist — concerning whose work he accepts the opinion of Moland and d'Héricault.[3]

---

[1] *G. Chaucer*, etc., Berlin, 1872, pp. 49 ff.

[2] *Comparison*, etc., p. iii.

[3] *l. c.*, pp. v.–vi. R. Fischer's *Die Troilus-Epen von Boc·*

In 1867 J. Koch expressed the opinion that Chaucer possessed Boccaccio's works, of which he made such liberal use in his own poems in a manuscript or manuscripts which did not give the name of the author, and in the case of the *Filostrato*, as in that of other works, in order to give it an author, attributed it to one Lollius, whose name he may have come upon in the lines of Horace, cited by Latham and ten Brink.[1]

In 1877 M. Landau, who supplemented Kissner's results by researches in the comparison of the English and Italian poems, noting that Chaucer had translated literally some 1200 verses of his original, advocated the view that the English

caccio und Chaucer (in *Zu den Kunstformen des mittelalterlichen Epos. Weiner Beiträge zur englischen Philologie*, vol. IX. (1899) pp. 217–370) offers nothing new on the question. It is a comparison of the æsthetic value of two poems, stated in percentages.

[1] *Englische Studien*, vol. I. pp. 291–292.

poet was ashamed to mention a modern writer in Italian as Boccaccio, and therefore had adopted a Latin name which he cited as his authority.[1]

Ten Brink, in his *Geschichte der Englischen Litteratur*, published in 1893, notes where Chaucer had made use of the work of Benoit at one point in his narrative, "Und begierig greift er aus Benoits Darstellung Züge auf, die zur Entschuldigung seiner Heldin gereichen können. Erst dem von Troilus verwundeten Diomed schenkt sie, von Mitgefühl geruhrt, ihr Herz; und der Untreue folgt die Reue auf dem Fusse," [2] and in discussing the sources of the *Legend of Good Women*, he calls attention to the fact that if in this poem Chaucer has preferred Guido as a source rather than Benoit, it is the opposite of what he did in the Troilus. [3]

[1] *Boccaccio*, pp. 92–94.
[2] *Geschichte*, vol. II. p. 95.   [3] *l.c.*, p. 116.

In 1892 Lounsbury, who seemed to think that the work of Guido was one of the English poet's sources for the *Legend*,[1] stated that "Chaucer knew nothing of Benoit."[2] In 1894 Skeat, who in earlier contributions, when he had occasion to touch on the subject, accepted without comment the views of others upon the *Filostrato-Troilus* and "Lollius" questions with his usual disregard of the antecedent work of others, writing as if he were the first to suggest the possible indebtedness of Chaucer to Guido, pointed out details in the *Troilus* which he thought had their origin in the Latin work, and cited a number of passages of the *Historia Trojana* from an inferior manuscript to prove his thesis. "Trophe," as mentioned by both Chaucer and Lydgate, according to

---

[1] *Studies in Chaucer*, vol. II. pp. 313–314.
[2] *l.c.*, vol. II. p. 309.

his view, was Guido's work;[1] but he did not fail to note where, in the *Troilus*, Chaucer was unquestionably indebted to the *Roman de Troie*.[2]

W. J. Courthope in his *History of English Poetry* regarded the use of Lollius as a deliberate mystification, on the part of Chaucer, to mislead his readers. As the authority of a work to which he wished to give a moral tone, Boccaccio "even if he had not provoked the censure of the church, would have carried no historical weight"; and "therefore to create for his imaginary history, an imaginary historian," he referred to "the Latin of the supposed Trojan historian Lollius." To fill out the story as he found it in the *Filostrato*, "he borrowed numerous incidents and touches of a highly dramatic kind

---

[1] *Works of Chaucer*, vol. II. pp. liii.–lxi.
[2] *l.c.*, pp. lxi.–lxii., lxxx.

E

from the *Historia Trojana* of Guido delle Colonne." [1]

Finally, J. W. Broatch, in an article [2] in which he is assuredly "amicus Platonis," totally denies the claims of the *Historia* as set forth by Skeat, as one of the joint sources of the English poem. Unfortunately he rests his case mainly upon his own arbitrary statements, which are not, and cannot be substantiated by citations from the work of either Benoit or Guido.

Of the known authors to whom Chaucer could have had recourse for the story of

[1] *Hist. of Eng. Poetry,* vol. I. pp. 262–263.

[2] *Journal of Germanic Philology,* vol. II. (1898) pp. 14–28. W. S. McCormick seems to accept Broatch's conclusion when he states, "For the development of the story in Book V. Chaucer evidently consulted the *Roman de Troie* of Benoit de Sainte-More, possibly also the *Historia Troiana* of Guido delle Colonne." *Globe Chaucer,* p. xli.; cf. pp. 543, 546, 553.

the *Troilus and Criseyde*, Guido delle Colonne[1] is the only one whom he mentions by name in any of his works. In the *Hous of Fame*,[2] in the list of the historians of Troy, he groups together

> "the great Omeer;
> And with him Dares and Tytus
> Before, and eek he, Lollius,
> And Guido eek de Columpnis;"

and by this mention of Lollius, removes any chance for the conjecture that by this name Guido was meant. Again, in his *Legend of Good Women*, at the beginning of the story of Hypsipyle and Medea, he mentions Guido as his authority.

"Tessalye, as Guido telleth us."[3]

---

[1] The name always appears as "de Columpnis" in autograph signatures: (F. Torraca, *Giornale Dantesco*, vol. V. pp. 271–277; *Studi su la lirica italiana del Duecento*, 1902, pp. 449–452), and in the best manuscripts of the *Historia*. [2] *H. of F.*, 1466–1469.

[3] *L. of G. W.*, 1396. Skeat was the first, in 1889, to restore the correct manuscript reading, "Guido," which

And when he leaves him to follow another author, he notifies his readers: —

> "Al be this not rehersed of Guido,
> Yet seith Ovyde in his Epistles so." [1]

A careful study of the subject has shown the truthfulness of the poet's statement, and pointed out his exact indebtedness to both the authors mentioned.[2]

had before always been printed as "Ovyde." The *Legend of Good Women*, 1889, pp. xxxi., 167. *Works of G. Chaucer*, 1894, vol. II. p. liv.

[1] *L. of G. W.*, 1464–1465.

[2] Bech, *Anglia*, vol. V. pp. 324, 329–330, on Guido as source; cf. *Legend of Good Women*, p. xxxi.; Lounsbury, *l.c.*, vol. II. p. 313; J. W. Broatch, *Journal of Germanic Philology*, vol. II. pp. 22–23. Chaucer, in following Guido, who substituted Ovid's " Thessalia " for Benoit's "Grece," perhaps to escape the difficulty found in the French poet's transformation of Dares's "Peloponneso " into "Penolope " (*R. de T.*, 712; on source of name in Dares, cf. Dunger, *l.c.*, p. 15; Koerting, *Dictys and Dares*, p. 73), which gave a Middle English translator trouble (*The Seege of Troye*, edited by C. H. A. Wager, 1889, v. 25; cf. p. lix.), although acquainted with Dares, does not, here or elsewhere (*L. of G. W.*, 1397, 1400, 1409; cf. p. 167), correct "Pelleus " into "Pelias " (cf. Hertzberg, *l.c.*, p. 121; Joly, *l.c.*, vol. I. p. 222, n.; H. Morf, *Rom*, vol. XXI. p. 89).

And in the *Hous of Fame* he refers anonymously to him as an authority for an opinion which he himself does not seem to accept.

> " But yit I gan ful wel espye,
> Betwix hem was a litel envye,
> Oon seyde, Omere made lyes,
> Feyninge in his poetryes,
> And was to Grekes favorable ;
> Therfor held he hit but fable." [1]

For in Benoit's poem there is no passage corresponding in the least to Guido's long invective against Homer.

After telling of the treacherous slaying of Troilus by his Greek opponent, Guido goes on : —

" Sed o homere qui in libris tuis achillem tot laudibus tot preconiis extulisti ; quæ probabilis ratio te induxit ut achillem tantis probitatis

Lydgate, who had followed others in this mistake in his *Troy-book*, repeats it in his *Tragedies* (sig. c 1 verso. col. 1).

[1] *H. of F.*, 1475–1480.

titulis exaltasses, ex eo precipue quod dixeris achillem ipsum suis viribus duos hectores peremisse ipsum videlecet et troilum fortissimum fratrem ejus. Sane si te induxit grecorum affectio a quibus originem diceris produxisse vera non motus diceris ratione, sed potius ex furore." [1]

---

[1] *Historia*, sig. l 2 verso, col. 2. Benoit's only comment on Homer (*R. de T.*, 45–66 = Dares, *De Excidio Troiœ*, ed. Meister, 1, 13–17) is to the effect that his statements could not be true, as he lived one hundred years after the Trojan war, and that the Athenians

> " Dampner le voldrent par raison
> Por ce qu'ot fet les Damedeus
> Conbatre o les homes charneus "

(*R. de T.*, 60–62; cf. Constans, *Revue des Universites du Midi*, vol. IV. pp. 36, 53), which Guido translated in its proper place. *Historia*, sig. a 1 recto, col. 1–2. It is of this passage that Broatch (*l.c.*, p. 20) writes, " Thus in 45 he sneers at the paganism of Homer," and of the closing lines of the poem, — a mere scribal formula, —

> " Celui gart Dex et tienge et voie
> Qui bien essauce et monteploie " —

(*R. de T.*, 30107–30108 *ed.*, " Qui bien s'avance et monteploie," but I have read as above on authority of MSS. B.N., 782, 1553; Arsenal, 3340, 3342) he remarks that the poet "expresses Christian sentiments." He emphasizes

In the *Monkes Tale* the stanza in the account of Hercules

" Was never wight, sith that the world bigan,
  That slow so many monstres as dide he.
  Thurgh-out this wyde world his name ran,
  What for his strengthe, and for his heigh
      bountee,
  And every reaume wente he for to see.
  He was so strong that no man mighte him
      lette;
  At bothe the worldes endes, seith Trophee,
  In stede of boundes, he a pilar sette." [1]

finds no analogue in the passage in Boethius in Chaucer's own translation,[2] which was so closely followed in the two preceding stanzas,[3] but has its source in Guido's state-

these passages as the only evidence to support his arbitrary statement that Chaucer could have found " his source in Benoit as well as in Guido " for his attack upon paganism (*T. and C.*, V. 1849–1855).

[1] *Canterbury Tales*, B, 3301–3307.

[2] *Boethius De Consolatione Philosophie*, Book IV. Metre VII. 29–67.

[3] *C. T.*, B, 3282–3300

ment, much enlarged upon that of Benoit, which merely has

"Et les bonnes ilec ficha." [1]

And Chaucer may have referred to this very statement, only in order to supplement it with the information he found in what he considered a better authority, in the work of Guido.

"Hic est ille hercules de cujus incredibilibus actibus per multas mundi partes sermo dirigitur. Qui sua potentia infinitos gigantes suis temporibus interemit . . . ista de eo sufficiant tetigisse cum et rei veritas in tantum de sua victoria acta per mundum miraculose divulget, quod usque in hodiernum diem usque quam victor apparuit columne herculis testentur ad gades." [2]

---

[1] *R. de T.*, 795.

[2] *Historia*, sig. a 3 recto, col. 1; cf. *R. de T.*, 791-794, 797-798 : —

> "Hercules
> Cil qui sostint maint pesant fes,
> Et mainte grant merveille fist.
> Et maint felon jaiant ocit."
> "Ses granz merveilles et si fait
> Serront mès à toz jorz retrait."

"Et locus ille in quo predicte columne Herculis sunt affixe — a quo non sufficit ultra ire." [1]

But Chaucer, in other poems where no authority is named, shows that he is well acquainted with Guido's work. In the *Book of the Duchesse* he dreams that on the windows of his room

> "hoolly al the storie of Troye
> Was in the glasing y-wrought thus,
> Of Ector and king Priamus,
> Of Achilles and Lamedon,
> Of Medea and of Jason,
> Of Paris, Eleyne, and Lavyne." [2]

---

[1] *Historia*, sig. a 3 recto, col. 2; cf. Skeat, *Works of Chaucer*, vol. II. p. lv. Yet Broatch (*l.c.*, 21) states that "the passage from the *Monk's Tale* . . . is found in Benoit." Cf. *R. de T.*, 796, "Ou Alexandres les [bonnes] trova," with Guido's "Ad has columnas magnas Macedonius Alexander . . . subjugando sibi mundum in manu legitur pervenisse," *Historia*, sig. a 3 recto, col. 1. Chaucer's "both the worldes endes," as well as the statement in Guido, is based upon the geographical misconception so often found in mediæval writers, which first confused, and finally made one, the Eastern "bornes" of Bacchus or Alexander, and the Western limits set by Hercules or Arthur. [2] *B. of D.*, 326–331.

In Guido's work especially is a prominent place given to the loves of Medea and Jason,[1] as a part of the Trojan story, and from this source the English poet took the names in this passage, as, at a later period, in the *Legend of Good Women*, he utilized the narrative.

Again, in the same poem, when we find:—

> " And therto al-so hardy be
> As was Ector, so have I joye,
> That Achilles slow at Troye —
> And therfor was he slayn also
> In a temple, for bothe two

[1] Cf. A. Joly, *l.c.*, vol. I. p. 474; Bech, *Anglia*, vol. V. p. 331. While Guido always writes " Hector," the aphæresized form, " Ector," appears in Benoit after *qu' d'*, etc. (*R. de T.*, 296, 371; 283, 394, 420); but this was a common O.F. form which Chaucer could have found elsewhere. Cf. " Ercules," *B. of D.*, 1058; and see p. 56. " Priamus " is exceptional in Benoit (Constans, *l.c.*, p. 67); " Lamedon " has no precedent in " Laomedon " of both authors; but for the manuscript reading, " king " before name which, it is true, may merely have been caught from *l.* 328, cf. " Li reis de Troi[e] Laomedon " (*R. de T.*, 989); " Rex Laomedon," *Historia*, sig. **a** 4 recto, col. 1. But the form " Laumedon," found both in

Were slayn, he and Antylegyus,
And so seyth Dares Frigius,
For love of [hir] Polixena." [1]

It is evidently a summing-up of the story
of the passion of Achilles for Polyxena,
such as it appeared, in an extended form,
in the *Historia* of Guido.[2] That Dares was
not the immediate source, as stated by
Chaucer, is conclusively demonstrated by
his forced spelling of the name " Antilogus," which Guido had taken as he
found it in Benoit,[3] who had thus distorted

Benoit (Constans, *l.c.*, pp. 34–35, where synæresis must
be allowed on account of the metre) and in Guido, would
give Chaucer's spelling of the name as "Laodamia,"
"Laudomia," which became "Ladomea."   Cf. *L. of G.
W.*, 924; *C. T.*, B, 71; F, 1445; cf. *T. and C.*, IV. 124,
"Lameadoun."   With "Lavyne" cf. *R. de la Rose*, ed.
Michel, 21818, "Helaine ne Lavine," but 14169, "Helaine,"
"Médée," *l.c.*, 14170, 15349.

[1] *B. of D.*, 1064–1071.   On spelling "Antilogus,"
Skeat, *Minor Poems of Chaucer*, 2d ed. p. 491.

[2] *Historia*, sig. k 2 verso, col. 1, — l 4 recto, col. 1; cf.
R. de T., 17457–18354, 19177–19289, 19395–19779, 20679–
20848, 21176–21256, 21799–22256.

[3] *R. de T.*, 585, 20969, 22091; *Historia*, sig. l 3 verso,
col. 2, — l 4 recto, col. 1.

the " Antilochus " of Dares.[1] And that it
was to Guido's, and not to Benoit's, work

[1] Dares, 41, 8; 11, 13. Skeat's statement (*Minor
Poems*, p. 266), "Antilochus is a mistake for Archilochus,
owing to the usual mediæval confusion of proper names,"
is not based on a single fact. Archilochus, who, in the
Iliad (XI. 100, XIV. 164), is the son of Antenor, in
Dares (23, 4) is a Thracian ally of the Trojans; in
Benoit (*R. de T.*, 6854, 7692) Archilogus is the son of
" Theseus de Theresche," and again appears in the same
rôle in the *Historia* (sig. f 6 recto, col. 1; g 3 recto,
col. 1) as "Artilogus" and "Archileus." But Guido,
misunderstanding a passage in Benoit (*R. de T.*, 8360–
8361, where " Antilogus " appears as the son of Theseus),
makes an " Artilogus " the son of another Theseus (*Historia*, g 5 recto, col. 2; cf. wrong translation again in the
Gest Hystoriale, ed. Paton and Donaldson, 6448–6450),
who in both writers appears as a Greek ally (*R. de T.*,
8179–8184, 8873–8902, 9045–9062, 11174; *Historia*, sig.
g 4 verso, col. 1; g 6 verso, col. 1; h 1 recto, col. 1). A
certain " Artilegus " is introduced by Guido — in a passage in which two episodes are made from one in Benoit
— as a doublet of " Archelaus," who is slain by Hector
(*Historia*, sig. h 5 recto, col. 2; cf. *R. de T.*, 10817 ff.). In
Lydgate's *Troy-book* (sig. X 2 verso, col. 2, but X 3 recto,
col. 2; verso, cols. 1–2, the correct form " Anthylogus "
appears), in the *Gest Hystoriale* (10555–10556), and the
La destruction de Troye of Milet (3987), Archilogus is the
son of Nestor; cf. *Works of Chaucer*, vol. VI. p. 401.

that Chaucer was directly indebted, is shown by the name of the author, " Dares Frigius," such as it appeared in the former;[1] while " Daires," " Daire," " Dares "[2] is a less specific nomenclature, found in the Old French poem.

Then in the lines, —

> " nay, certes, than were I wel
> Wers than was Achitofel,
> Or Anthenor, so have I joye,
> The traytour that betraysed Troye, "[3]

is at once the mediæval tradition and spelling of Antenor, such as we find in Guido,[4] and when Chaucer writes, —

---

[1] *Historia*, sig. e 1 verso, col. 1; e 3 recto, col. 1; f 5 verso, col. 1; cf. p. 70 n.

[2] *R. de T.*, 2048, 2051, 3107, 12292, 14048, 16210, 21395, 21173 ; 106, 5183, 9957, 23722; Constans, *l.c.*, p. 68.   On Chaucer's acquaintance with the work of Dares, when writing the *L. of G. W.*, Bech, *Anglia*, vol. V. pp. 325–326.   [3] *B. of D.*, 1117–1120.

[4] *Historia*, sig. m 1 recto, col. 1 ff.; cf. *R. de T.*, 24373–26325.   There is no hint anywhere in Chaucer's works to show that he accepted the mediæval conception

> "Allas that day
> The sorwe I suffred, and the wo !
> That trewlwy Cassandra, that so
> Bewayled the destruccioun
> Of Troye and of Ilioun,
> Had never swich sorwe as I tho," [1]

he follows Guido in making a distinction between Troy and Ilium,[2] and, as he, gives Cassandra, who is only incidentally men-

of Æneas as a traitor in conjunction with Antenor, in contradiction to the narrative of Virgil (cf. *H. of F.*, 162 ff.; *L. of G. W.*, 930 ff.), unless it be in the line in the *Troilus* (II. 1474) in which the two are named together as friends of the enemy of Criseyde, "Were it for Antenor and Eneas," a juxtaposition of names to be found in Benoit (299; 24373). Nor is the story that Simon entered Troy concealed in the wooden horse, — in Guido one of brass, "equum erum " — found in his mediæval authorities (*R. de T.*, 25618–25639, 25760–25923; *Historia*, sig. m 4 verso, col. 2 — m 5 recto, col. 1), accepted to the rejection of the Virgilian authority. (*H. of F.*, 151–155; *L. of G. W.*, 930–933; *C. T.*, B, 4418–4419; F, 209–211, 305–307) ; cf. *Works of Chaucer*, V. p. 377.

[1] *B. of D.*, 1243–1249.

[2] *Historia*, sig. c 2 verso, col. 1–2, in the section treating of the building of Troy by Priam, we find : —

tioned in the narrative of the *Æneid*,[1] a prominent position in the Trojan story.[2]

Ilion formari constituit quod magnum ejus palacium appelatur.

Again in the section *De direptione Troie* we find after entering the city that

Greci . . . in magnum ilion irruerunt

(sig. m 6 recto, col. 1). The same distinction is made in the *H. of F.*, 152, 155, 158; and in the *L. of G. W.*, 936–937, —

"In al the noble tour of Ilioun
That of the citee was the cheef dungeoun,"

not only the distinction, but the language, is taken from Benoit, *R. de T.*, 3029–3030 (cf. 645–646, 10366, 24316–24317, 25275, 26029, 26119).

"A une part font Ylion
De Troie le mestre danjon,"

Broatch, *l.c.* p. 22; cf. Fromman, *Germania*, vol. II. p. 77; *C. T.*, B, 288–289, 4546.

[1] *Æn.*, II. 246, 403; III. 187; V. 636.

[2] *Historia*, sig. C 1 verso, col. 1 = *R. de T.*, 2941–2942 = *Dares*, 6, 4; *Historia*, sig. e 2 recto, col. 2 = *R. de T.*, 4127–4144 = *Dares*, 11, 2–5; *Historia*, sig. o 6 recto, col. 2 = *R. de T.*, 4861–4916 = *Dares*, 13, 14–16; *Historia*, sig. e 3 recto, col. 1 = *R. de T.*, 5509–5520 = *Dares*, 15, 17–18; *Historia*, sig. h 3 verso, col. 1 = *R. de T.*, 10355–10390; *Historia*, sig. m 4 verso, col. 2 = *R. de T.*, 25482–25488; *Historia*, sig. m 5 verso, col. 2 =

In the list of lovers in the *Parlement of Foules,* —

" Tristram, Isoude, Paris, and Achilles,
    Eleyne, Cleopatre, and Troilus," [1]

the heroes of the two romantic episodes of the *Historia* are alluded to ; in the line of the *Legend of Good Women,* —

" And Polixene, that boghten love so dere," [2]

R. de T., 26009–26019 = *Dares,* 49, 21–50, 17; *Historia,* sig. m 6 recto, col. 1 = *R. de T.,* 26107–26112. In these passages her seer's powers are mentioned, and her prophetic lamentations are set forth in full.

[1] *P. of F.,* 290–291. J. Koch (*Englischen Studien,* vol. I. pp. 284–285) thinks that these lines, in which Troilus is taken as a type of a lover, could only have been written after Chaucer had become acquainted with the *Filostrato,* as his story only forms a minor episode in the works of Benoit and Guido. But he leaves unexplained the introduction of Achilles, whose name, however, as that of Cleopatra, Paris, and Tristram, the English poet may have taken from a passage in the *Divina Commedia* of Dante (*Inf.,* V. 63–67), of which the *P. of F.* shows the earliest influence. Cf. *Inf.,* II. 1–3, 83–84, 10–11, 19–20; *Purg.,* XXVIII., 16–18, 7–9, with *P. of F.,* 85–86, 109–112, 123–124, 141, 169–170, 201–203.   [2] *L. of G. W.,* B, 258.

there is again a reference to one of these; in the *Nonne Preestes Tale* one of the "ensamples," to illustrate the value of dreams cited by Chauntecleer, —

> "Lo heer Andromacha, Ectores wyf,
> That day that Ector sholde lese his lyf,
> She dremed on the same night biforn,
> How that the lyf of Ector sholde be lorn,
> If thilke day he wente in-to bataille ;
> She warned him, but it mighte nat availle ;
> He wente for to fighte nathelees,
> But he was slayn anoon of Achilles,
> But thilke tale is al to long to telle,
> And eek it is ny day, I may nat dwelle," [1]

which has no classical authority, can be found in the narrative of Guido. So far as the evidence of the names in the first passage goes, Chaucer may have already become acquainted with the work of Benoit; he makes use of the old French poem, as well as of the Latin romance, elsewhere in the

[1] *C. T.*, B., 4331–4340.

F

Legend of Good Women,[1] and in either of these works he could have read the story of the fate of Polyxena, who was slain at the tomb of Achilles by Pyrrhus, because for her —

"sis peres fu ocis."[2]

Again, in the summary of the dream of Andromache and its fulfilment there is no hint in its details or language upon which it can be stated conclusively whether it was to the narrative of Benoit or to that of Guido, Chaucer was indebted.[3]

[1] Cf. p. 52, n. 2; p. 62, n. 2.

[2] *R. de T.,* 26297; cf. 663–668, 26369–26432; *Historia,* sig. m 6 verso, col. 1 — n 1, recto, col. 1. For phrase, "boghten love so dere," cf. *T. and C.,* I., 810: "Many a man hath love ful dere y-bought," which has no equivalent in the parallel passage of the *R. de la R.,* 21878; but *T. and C.,* V. 1755–1756; "His ire . . . the Grekes ay boughte," V. 1800–1801; "The wraththe . . . of Troilus the Grekes boughten dere," finds its counterpart in Benoit's "Chier lo comparent Troien" (23688); "Cil de là l'ont chier comparée" (21204); "Mes trop les a, chier comparé" (20122). Cf. 17944, 668, 13290.

[3] *R. de T.,* 15187 ff.; cf. 390–412; *Historia,* sig. i 4

In taking the *Filostrato* as a basis for his Troilus, Chaucer, knowing both of the works from which Boccaccio drew the rudiments of his story,[1] did not hesitate to adopt

verso, col. 2 ff., where name as elsewhere in the same work is spelled Andrometa. Tyrwhitt had stated (*l.c.*, p. 204, note to l. 15147), " The first author who relates it is the fictitious Dares, cxxiv, and Chaucer very probably took it from him, or from Guido de Columnis, or perhaps from Benoit de Sainte More." Cf. Broatch (*l.c.*, p. 22), "Tyrwhitt affirmed that the dream of Andromache . . . came from Guido. It might as well have come from Benoit."

[1] Le Clerc was of the opinion that " le *Filostrato* n'est qu'un développement de l'épisode de Troilus et Briséida ou Criséida dans le poëme française de la Guerre de Troie par Benoît de Sainte-More " (*Hist. litt. de la France*, vol. XXIV. pp. 553–554). Hortis (*Studi sulle opere latine del Boccaccio*, 1879, p. 118), Sandras (*l.c.*, p. 42), Moland and d'Hericault (*l.c.*, p. xciii), and Barth (*Guido de Columna*, Leipzig, 1877, p. 34) do not try to decide whether it was to Benoit or Guido that Boccaccio was indebted for the story of the Troilus. G. Koerting (*Boccaccios Leben und Werke*, 1880, p. 590) and V. Cresini (*Contributo agli studi sul Boccaccio*, 1887, p. 195) widen the question by the suggestion that it may have been taken from an Italian translation of either Benoit or Guido, instead of from the original of either

hints from those authors which had been neglected by Boccaccio. Not only did he dovetail into his own narrative details of the Latin and French versions of the Troilus episode which had been omitted or changed by the Italian writer, but also followed " myn auctor " in seeking material in other episodes, and weaving romances about names found in their common authorities. And in such additions from Benoit and Guido the predominance of the former as an authority is evident both in

(cf. C. H. A. Wager, *The Seege of Troye*, p. xxii.).   Dunger (*l.c.*, p. 36), Hertzberg (*l.c.*, p. 200), Bartoli (*Iprecursori del Boccaccio*, 1876, pp. 64–66; cf. 70–80), M. Landau (*Giovanni Boccaccio; seine Leben und seine Werke*, 1877, pp. 90–91), and Gorra (*Testi inediti di storia troiana*, etc., 1889, p. 339 ff.) believed that Guido's original text was the direct source; while Joly (*l.c.*, vol. I. p. 504), Gaspary (*Gesch. der italienischen Lit.*, vol. II. p. 638), Morf (*Rom.*, vol. XXI. p. 106), and Savj-Lopez (*Rom*, vol. XXVII. pp. 445–449) attributed the greater influence to Benoit, although acknowledging the supplementary use of Guido; and Savez-Lopez was the first (*l.c.*, pp. 451–453) to note Boccaccio's indebtedness to the love episode of Achilles in Benoit.

language and sentiment, while he accepts the statements of the latter for specific details, the correctness of which he thinks can be vouched for. While Benoit always writes for Dictys, "Dithis"[1] or "Ditis,"[2] Guido in translating the passage in the French poem which tells of the discovery by Cornelius, the "neveu" of "Saluistes,"[3] of —

> "L'estoire que Daire ot escrite
> Et en langue greçoise dite,"[4]

regarded the participle "dite" as a proper name, and, here and elsewhere, always

[1] *R. de T.*, 637, 24301, 26202, 30095.

[2] *R. de T.*, 24299, 24322, 26040; Constans, *l.c.*, p. 64.

[3] *R. de T.*, 77–79.

> "Cist Saluistes, ço truis lisant
> Ot un neveu forment sachant
> Cornelius fu apelez,"

is Benoit's interpretation of the words in the formula of address, "Cornelius Nepos Sallustio," in Dares. Cf. Joly, *l.c.*, vol. I. p. 477.

[4] *R. de T.*, 87–88, ed. "En greque langue fete et dite," which I have rejected in favor of the reading in Vienna 2571, *ap.* G. K. Fromman, *Germania*, vol. II. p. 62.

referred to this author, with whose work
he was unacquainted, as Dites,[1] so, Chaucer,
whose ignorance on this point was one with
Guido, names " Dyte " as a writer on the
Trojan war, and when he gives the advice,

" But the Troiane gestes, as they felle,
In Omer, or in Dares, or in Dyte,
Who-so that can, may rede hem as they wryte,"[2]

he is speaking in all seriousness to those
who were better situated than he.   That
he came to doubt the authority that he
accepted when writing the *Troilus* is
shown in the later poem, *The Hous of*

[1] *Historia*, sig. a 1 recto, col. 2.

" Eaque per ditem grecum et frigius Daretem . . . in
presentem libellum per me judicem Guidonem de columnis
messana transsumpta legentur, prout in duobus libris
eorum inscriptum, quasi una vocis consonantis inventum
est athenis.   Quamquam autem hos libellos . . . Cornelius
nomine Salustii magni nepos in latinam transferre
curverit."

This mistake of Guido was first noted by Hertzberg,
l.c., 189–190.   Cf. sig. o. 7 recto, col. 1, " ditem grecum."
On passage in epilogue, *Historia*, sig. O 6 recto, col. 2, in
which the form " ditis " occurs — which may be only a
gloss, cf. H. Morf (*Rom*, vol. XXI. pp. 20-21).

[2] *T. and C.*, I. 145–147.

Fame, where, again in a list of writers on Troy, he names
"the great Omere,
And with him Dares and Tytus." [1]

This is no mere spelling of a name, but the statement of a correction to which the poet had given thought.   In his readings he had not come across the work of "Ditis — Dithis—Dites," and to attribute such a work to a well-known historian, "Tytus Livius," [2] one of whose names could easily have been corrupted, seemed the sensible way.

Chaucer was so well acquainted with the story of Achilles and Polyxena [3] that he

---

[1] *H. of F.*, 1466–1467.

[2] *B. of the D.*, 1084=*R. de la R.*, 9365; *L. of G. W.*, A, 280. 1873, (Titus) 1683; *C. T.*, C, 1.   In the *B. of the D.* the allusion to Lucretia is only at second hand, in the *L. of G. W.* the Latin history was used as a source, while again in the *Frankeleyns Tale*, where no authority is named, the name occurs in the list of virtuous women, translation from the monastic tract *Contra Jovinianum*. Cf. *C. T.*, F, 1405–1409; Migne, *Patrologia*, vol. XXIII. col. 275.   [3] Cf. p. 59.

recognized the use made of it by Boccaccio in telling of the beginning of the love adventures of Troilus, and enlarged his own narrative by hints drawn from both of the sources of the Italian poet.

Boccaccio's lines, —

"il quale [*i.e.* Troilus] amore trafisse
Piu ch'alcun altro,"[1]

could hardly have been the original of Chaucer's longer and more specific statement, —

"the god of love gan loken rowe
Right for despyt, and shoop for to ben wroken;
He kidde anoon his bowe nas not broken;
For sodeynly he hit him at the fulle;"[2]

while the figure employed seems to suggest the use of a passage in Guido's description of the first meeting of Achilles and Polyxena : —

"Et dum desirabili animo in eam Achilles suum infixisset intuitum sagitta cupidimis for-

---

[1] *Fil.*, I. 25, 7–8.　　　　[2] *T. and C.*, I. 206–209.

tem Achillem subito vulneravit et ad interiora pertransiens cordis ejus." [1]

Again, Chaucer's lines,

" And sodeynly he wex ther-with astoned,
And gan hire bet biholde in thrifty wyse:
' O mercy, god!' thoughte he, ' wher hastow
    woned,
Thou art so fair and goodly to devyse ? ' " [2]

" And after that hir loking gan she lighte,
That never thoughte him seen so good a sighte.
And of hir look in him ther gan to quiken
So greet desir, and swich affeccioun,
That in his hertes botme gan to stiken
Of hir his fixe and depe impressioun :
And though he erst hadde poured up and doun,
He was tho glad his hornes in to shrinke;
Unnethes wiste he how to loke or winke," [3]

which have no parallel in the *Filostrato*, are a clever piecing together of unconnected

---

[1] *Historia*, sig. k 2 verso, col. 2. Cf. E. Meybrinck, *Die Auffassung der Antike bei Jacques Milet, Guido de Columna und Benoît de Saint-Maur*, Marburg, 1886, p. 46.

[2] *T. and C.*, I. 274–278.

[3] *T. and C.*, I. 293–301.

expressions in the Latin Romance in the same episode : —

" Achilles igitur dum Polixenam inspexit et ejus pulchritudinem contemplatus vere suo concepit in animo nunquam se vidisse puellam nec aliquam mulierem tante pulchritudinis forma vigere. . . . Qui dum in eam frequentius intuendo sibi ipsi placere putaret et lenire grave desiderium cordis sui majoris scissure cordis vulneris seipsum sibi reddebat actorem. . . . Quid ultra Amore Polixene nimium, illaqueatus, Achilles nescit ipse quid faciat. . . . Propter quod dilatat amplius plagas suas et sui amoris vulnera magis sui cordis attrahit in profundum." [1]

---

[1] *Historia*, sig. k 2 verso, col. 2, — k 3 recto, col. 1; cf. Gower, *Conf. Amant.* V. 7591 ff.   The lines,

> [Calchas]
> " Knew wel that Troye sholde destroyed be,
> By answere of his god, that highte thus,
> Daun Phebus or Apollo Delphicus,
>
> (T. and C., I. 68–70)
>
> Thus shal I seyn, and that his coward herte
> Made him amis the goddes text to glose,
> When he for ferde out of his Delphos sterte,"
>
> (T. and C., IV. 1409–1411)

in which there is an allusion to the journey of Calchas to

Boccaccio did not give a description of Troilus, and Chaucer, in combining details from Benoit and Guido, takes his more definite information from the latter. Thus, when Pandarus refers to

> " Troilus
> The wyse worthy Ector the secounde,"[1]

the Delphic oracle in the interests of the Trojans, the warning of the god, which he obeyed, in accompanying Achilles to Athens, — not a suggestion of which appears in the *Filostrato*, — do not furnish any hint as to whether it was to the French or the Latin work (cf. *R. de T.*, 5809–5918; *Historia*, sig. e 6 recto, col. 1) Chaucer had resort to at this point in the story. However, it may be noted that Phebus with the French epithet does not appear in the *R. de T.* (cf. Danz Apollin, 13732) nor does the Latin "Delphicus" appear in Guido (" Apollo," *Historia*, sig. e 5 verso, col. 2). Lydgate accepts the authority of Chaucer, and in his translation of this passage we find " Apollo Delphicus" (*Troy-book*, sig. 2 recto, col. 2). Guido confused Delos and "Delphos insulam" (*Historia*, sig. e 4 recto, col. 2; e 5 verso, col. 2). Benoit has Defeis (*R. de T.*, 205, 5786). Chaucer may have written Delphos on the authority of Dares (19, 13 and 19). Cf. *C. T.*, F, 1077, " Thy temple in Delphos wol I barefoot seke." The account of Calchas in the *Filostrato* (I. 8–9) corresponds to the more general statement of Guido in another passage (*Historia*, sig. i 1 recto, col. 2; cf. *R. de T.*, 12952 ff.).

[1] *T. and C.*, II. 157–158.

or when the poet speaking in his own
person says, —

"And certainly in storie it is y-founde,
 That Troilus was never un-to no wight,
 As in his tyme, in no degree secounde
 In durring don that longeth to a knight.
 Al mighte a geaunt passen him of might,
 His herte ay with the firste and with the beste
 Stod paregal, to durre don that him leste," [1]

we have two separate passages based upon
the statement in the *Historia:* —

"In viribus vero et strenuitate bellandi vel
fuit alius Hector vel secundus ab ipso. In toto
etiam regno Troie juvenis nullus fuit tantis
viribus nec tanta audacia gloriosus." [2]

---

[1] *T. and C.*, V. 834–840. Cf. II. 643, 739–740; III.
1774–1775; V. 1564–1565, 1803–1804.

[2] *Historia*, sig. e 2 verso, col. 1; cf. sig. k 6 recto,
col. 2,

"alius hector qui non minori predictus est virtute inclitus
ille scilicet troilus qui non minus quam si hector viveret,
grecos afficit"

= *R. de T.* (19890–19905; cf. 3973–3976, 5419–5421)
which again has its source in Dares (36, 20–22), "Dio-

In describing the sorrowful plight in
which Pandarus found Criseyde, Chaucer
availed himself of all that the *Filostrato*
offered, —

> " El vide lei in sul letto avviluppata
>   Ne' singhiozzi, nel pianto et ne' sospiri ;
>   E'l petto tutto et la faccia bagnata
>   Di lacrime le vide, ed in disiri
>   Di pianger gli occhi suoi, e scapigliata,
>   Dar vero segno degli aspri martiri," [1]

medes et Ulixes dicere coeperunt Troilum non minus
quam Hectorem virum fortissimum esse." Cf. Skeat,
l.c., p. lvi.; Broatch, *l.c.*, p. 16.   Skeat, *l.c.*, pp. lvi.–lvii.,
compares *T. and C.*, I. 1072–1085, with Guido's description of Troilus, while Broatch (*l.c.*, p. 16), noting that
these lines refer especially to the change that took place
in Troilus in consequence of his love, says that any
details in this passage " might equally well have been
taken from Benoit, 5372 ff."   But in fact Chaucer merely
anticipates the situation that he translates from the *Filostrato* in a later passage.   Cf. *T. and C.*, III. 1716–1729 ;
Fil., III. 72 ;   *T. and C.*, III. 1772–1778, 1786–1792 ; *Fil.*,
III. 90, 92.

   [1] *Fil.*, IV. 96. 1–6.   Cf. IV. 100, 7–8 : —

> " E intorno agli occhi un purpurino giro
>   Dava vero segnal del suo martiro,"

and by making his own a further detail in
Guido's description of the heroine's actions,
not put to use by Boccaccio,

" et aureos crines suos a lege ligaminis absolutos
divellit," [1]

introduced additional matter in his version, —

" And fond that she hir-selven gan to trete
    Ful pitously; for with hir salte teres
    Hir brest, hir face y-bathed was ful wete;

with *T. and C.*, IV. 869–870, —

        " About her eyen two a purple ring
            Bi-trent in sothfast tokninge of hir peyne."

The ultimate source is Dante (*Vita Nuova*, ch. xl.),
" Dintorno loro (*i.e.* gli occhi) si facea un colore purpu-
reo, lo quale suole apparir per alcuno martirio ch' altri
riceva,"

            " Ch' Amore
        Li cerchia di corona di martiri."

On indebtedness of the *Filostrato* to the *Vita Nuova*, cf.
Savj-Lopez in *Rom*, XXVII. pp. 443–444.

    [1] *Historia*, sig. i 2 recto, col. 2.   " Aureos crines suos
. . . divellit" = *Fil.*, IV. 87, 7 = *T. and C.*, IV. 736–737;
"ounded hair," cf. *R. de la R.*, 22131–22132; *H. of F.*,
1386.

The mighty tresses of hir sonnish heres,
Unbroyden, hangen al aboute hir eres ;
Which yaf him verray signal of martyre
Of deeth, which that hir herte gan desyre,"[1]

and it was the same phrase in Guido's
work that may have suggested to Chaucer,
in his description of Criseyde, the lines, —

" And ofte tyme this was hir manere,
To gon y-tressed with hir heres clere
Doun by hir coler at hir bak bihinde,
Which with a threde of gold she wolde binde."[2]

---

[1] *T. and C.*, IV. 813–819; *l.* 819 "her herte," *var.* "for
wo she."

[2] *T. and C.*, V. 809–812. A point suggested by Skeat
(*l.c.*, p. lvii.), although "this seems fantastic " to Broatch
(*l.c.*, pp. 17–18). The hint for this detail in the description
of Criseyde may be due to Guido, but the lines are only
a modification of a passage in the *P. of F.*, 267–268 : —

    " Her gilte heres with a golden threde
      Ybounded were, untressed as she lay,"

a free translation of the Italian original (*Tesaide*, VII.
65, 1–2), —

    " Ella avea d' oro i crini, et relegati
      Intorno al capo senza trecci alcuna."

But on the other hand, when he writes, —

"And eek her fingres longe and smale
She wrong ful ofte."

"Hir hewe, whylom bright, that tho was pale,"[1]

there is only a reminiscence of Guido's
stronger language : —

"Unguibus etiam suis sua tenerrima ora dila-
cerabat . . . et dum rigidis unguibus suas max-
illas exarat rubeo cruore, pertinctas, lacerata
lilia lacerata rosis immisceri similitudinarie
videbantur."[2]

A phrase of Guido's that suggested to
Chaucer in his version an addition to Boccaccio's description of the heroine has
already been noticed, and further, a com-

---

[1] *T. and C.*, IV. 737–738, 740.   Cf. *T. and C.*, V. 708,

"Full pale y-waxen was hir brighte face"

= *Fil.*, VI. 1, 6–7,

"le fresche guance et delicate
Pallide e magre l'eran divenute."

[2] *Historia*, sig. i 2, recto, col. 2; cf. *l.c.*, cols. 1–2, "si
promentis alicus [vestes] manibus strigerentur et aqua-
rum multitudinem effunderent."

parison of the analogous passages of the three authors shows that the English poet deferred to the authority of Guido when in conflict with that of Boccaccio — in this instance for artistic reasons if for no other cause. Thus, while Boccaccio tells us of his Griseida, that —

> " Ell' era grande, ed alla sua grandezza
> Rispondean bene i membri tutti quanti," [1]

Chaucer writes, —

> " Criseyde mene was of hir stature,"

in this as in his other lines, —

> " Thereto of shap, of face, and eek of chere
> There mighte been no fairer creature," [2]

> " And, save her browes joyneden y-fere,
> Ther nas no lak, in ought I can espyen," [3]

[1] *Fil.*, I. 27, 1–2, used by Chaucer in his description of Troilus (*T. and C.*, V. 827–828), which is similar to that given in *R. de T.*, 5405–5406, for which there is no equivalent in the *Historia* (sig. e 2 verso, col. 1). Cf. Skeat., *l.c.*, pp. lvi., lix.; Broatch, *l.c.*, pp. 16, 18, 26.

[2] *T. and C.*, V. 806–808.   [3] *T. and C.*, V. 813–814.

G

following the passage in Guido : —

"Breseida autem filia Calcas multa fuit spe-
ciositate decora nec longa nec brevis nec nimium
macilenta, lacteo profusa candore, genis roseis,
flavis crinibus. Sed superciliis junctis, quorum
junctura dum multa piloxitate tumesceret modi-
cam inconvenientam presentabat." [1]

[1] *Historia*, sig. e 2 recto, col. 1 ; cf. Dares, 17, 7–9,
"Briseidam formosam non alta *statura* . . . superciliis
junctis," and *R. de T.*, 5258, 5261–5262 : —

> "N'ert trop petite ne trop granz."
> "Mès le sorcil qui li giseient
> Auquetes li mesaveneient."

A single word in the first line suggests Dares as the
source, but his statement as to Criseyde's height is not
as definite as that of Benoit and Guido ; and only in the
Historia is the defect of the eyebrows emphasized. On
the other hand, it is to be noted that in Chaucer's story,
as in Boccaccio's, the heroine appears as a widow (*Fil.*,
I. 11, 3 = *T. and C.*, I. 97; cf. *Fil.*, I. 19, 2, with *T. and
C.*, I. 170; *Fil.*, II. 69, 2; *T. and C.*, II. 750 ff.; *Fil.*,
VI. 29, 1–3; *T. and C.*, V. 875–876), and although Chaucer states (*T. and C.*, I. 132–133) : —

> "But whether that she children hadde or noon,
> I rede it nought, therefore I lete it goon,"

Boccaccio specifically states that she did not have any
(*Fil.*, I. 15, 4–7; II. 69, 3; cf. W. S. McCormick,

For the expansion of the story of the wooing of Diomedes, Chaucer drew largely from the French poem, but in the answer of Criseyde, for the lines, —

> " I sey not therefore that I wol yow love,
> Ne I sey not nay, but in conclusioun
> I mene wel, by god that sit above," [1]

no specific analogous passage is found there, while in the Latin romance we find the passages of the same import, in which the

Globe Chaucer, p. 440); while Benoit (*R. de T.*, 12977) refers to her as "la pucele." There is no hint of her condition in either Guido or Dares; cf. Hertzberg, *l.c.*, pp. 197–198.

With *T. and C.*, V. 815–817 : —

> " But for to speken of hir eyen clere,
> Lo trewely, they writen that hir syen
> That Paradys stood formed in hir yën,"

cf. Dares, 17, 9, "oculis venustis"; *R. de T.*, 5263, " Biax ielz avoit de grant maniere " (cf. p. 124, n. 1); *Historia*, sig. e 2 recto, col. 2, "oculis venusta" (cf. Hertzberg, *l.c.*, p. 180, n.) ; *Fil.*, I. 28, 8, "Gli occhi lucenti e l'angelico viso"; *T. and C.*, V. 820–825 = *Fil.*, I. 11, 7; *R. de T.*, 5264–5270.

[1] *T. and C.*, V. 1002–1004.

thought and language is similar to what we find in the *Troilus:* —

"Amoris tui oblationes ad presens nec repudio nec admitto." [1]

"Unde sua calliditate se nolle non negat et velle in expectationis fiduciam conatur ponere Diomedem." [2]

But it was in Benoit's work alone that Chaucer found mention of the tokens of love that Criseyde presented to Diomedes, circumstances omitted by Guido, and so

[1] *Historia*, sig. i 2 verso, col. 1.

[2] *Historia*, sig. i 4 verso, col. 2. Skeat (*l.c.*, p. lx.) citing from MS., Mm. 5. 14, in Cambridge University Library, quotes the much closer analogue, "Unde Diomedi suum non negat, etiam nec promittit," but here as elsewhere I prefer the text, otherwise fuller and more correct, given in the incunabula. The lines in Benoit (15588–15589, 13641), —

> "N'est biau ne bien, reson ne dreiz
> Que d'amer vos donge parole,"

> "Gie ne vos refuse autrement,"

do not seem to support Broatch's statement (*l.c.*, p. 18), "There is nothing here which might not have come from Benoit."

changed in detail by Boccaccio, who had adopted this hint from this episode upon which to base an incident in his story, as to be hardly recognizable,[1] and the soliloquy of the heroine before she finally gives herself up to her Grecian lover,[2] omitted by Boccaccio, and very shortly summarized by Guido. And yet here in one line, —

"Retorning in hir soule ay up and doun,"[3]

Chaucer adopts a phrase of Guido's, —

"in sua mente revolvit,"[4]

[1] Cf. p. [2] *R de T.*, 20194–20330.
[3] *T. and C.*, V. 1023.
[4] *Historia*, sig. 1 recto, col. 1, but cf. *T. and C.*, II. 601–602: —
　　"And every word gan up and doun to winde,"
which translates the Italian, (*Fil.* II. 68, 3–4): —
　　"Seco nel cuor ciascuna paroletta
　　Rivolendo di Pandaro,"
which is rendered again in *T. and C.*, II. 659: —
　　"And gan to caste and rollen up and doun,"
while *T. and C.*, III. 1541–1542: —
　　"And in his thought gan up and doun to winde
　　Hir wordes alle,"

and, for brevity's sake, gives the gist of
Guido's account of the subsequent action
of the heroine, which is only implied in
the passage of the *Roman de Troie*. In
Guido's statement, —

"Totum suum animum in Diomedem declinat
et convertit amorem. Sed quam primum con-
valescentia adeptus absolute facere velle suum,
cum in ejus amore tota deferveat et flagranti
desiderio penitus incalescat,"[1]

Chaucer found authority for his lines : —

"And for to hele him of his sorwes smerte
Men seyn, I not, that she yaf him her herte."[2]

renders *Fil.*, III. 54, 1–2 : —

"E giva ciascun atto rivolgendo
Nel suo pensuiero."

[1] *Historia*, sig. l 1 recto, col. 1 ; cf. *R. de T.*, 20218–
20220 : —

"Desor puet l'en aperceveir
Que vers lui a tot atorné
S'amor, son cuer et son pensé."

[2] *T. and C.*, V. 1049–1050. Broatch, *l.c.*, p. 25, cites a
line of the heroine's speech (*R. de T.*, 20271), "Trop ai

A careful investigation of Guido's work, in conjunction with the other two sources, puts beyond doubt the truthfulness of the poet's statement when he writes, —

> " But trewely, how longe it was betwene,
> That she for-sook him for this Diomede
> Ther is non auctor telleth it, I wene,
> Take every man now to his bokes hede ;
> He shall no terme finden out of drede." [1]

But when he finds the exact number of days stated upon another matter, he is not so careful to follow his authorities.   For when he writes, —

> " For which, with-outen any wordes mo,
> To Troye I wol, as for conclusioun.
> But god it wot, er fully monthes two,
> She was ful fer fro that entencioun,
> For both Troilus and Troye town,

en lui ja mon cuer mie," which has at least one word which is in the English lines.

[1] *T. and C.*, V. 1086–1090.

Shall knotteles through-out hir herte slyde ; [1]
For she wol take a purpos for t'abyde," [2]

he flatly contradicts Guido's more radical
statement : —

"Non dum illa dies [*i.e.* the day of her arrival
in the Greek camp] ad horam declinaverat ves-
pertinam cum Briseida suas recentes mutaverat
voluntates et vetera proposita sui cordis, et jam
magis sibi succedit ad votum esse cum Grecis
quam fuisse hactenus cum Trojanis.   Jam
nobilis Troili amor cepit in sua mente tepescere
et tam brevi hora repente sic subito facta
volubilis ceperat in omnibus variari." [3]

---

[1] Cf. *Fil.*, VI. 8, 6–7 : —

> " E'n breve spazio ne cacciò di fuore
> Troilo e Troia, ed ogni altro pensiero
> Che'n lei fosse di lui o falso o vero."

[2] *T. and C.*, V. 764–770.   Cf. V. 912, 1006–1008, for
which the *Filostrato* does not furnish an analogue.

[3] *Historia*, sig. i 3 recto, col. 2.   Cf. *R. de T.*, 13823–
13827 : —

> " Anceis que venist le quart seir
> N'ot el corage, ne voleir
> De retorner en la cité

In the three lines which describe the
death of Hector is a phrase of which the
syntactical position, which offers difficulty,
is best explained by a comparison with the
parallel passage in Guido : —

" For as he drough a king by th' aventayle,
Unwar of this, Achilles through the mayle
And through the body gan him ryve." [1]

> Son corage est molt tost mué
> Poi veritable et poi estable."

Cf. *Fil.*, VI. 9, 1 = *T. and C.*, V. 842.   Cf. also *R. de T.*,
13403–13408; Constans *Chrestomathie de l'ancien française*,
1884, p. 62, *ll.* 169 ff., a mere general statement in which
Broatch (*l.c.*, p. 18) somehow finds the same definite statement as in Guido.   Lydgate in his *Troy-book* (sig. R
3 verso, col. 1–2), refers his readers to Chaucer's poem
for the complete story of Troilus and Criseyde, who are
only incidentally mentioned in Guido's narrative, but on
this one point introduces the statement of the *Historia* in
a garbled form : —

> " But Guydo sayth longe or it was nyght,
> How Cryseyde hath forsake her owne knight
> And gave her herte unto this Diomode,
> Of tendernesse and of womanhede."

[1] *T. and C.*, V. 1558–1560.

"Achilles . . . accepta quadam lancea valde forti *non advertente Hectore*, velociter in Hectorem irruit." [1]

Finally, when in one of his closing stanzas, —

"Lo here, of Payens corsed olde rytes,
Lo here, what alle hir goddes may availle;
Lo here, these wrecched worldes appetytes;

[1] *Historia*, sig. i 6 recto, col. 1; cf. l 3 recto, col. 1.   The rest of the passage is due to Benoit., *R. de T.*, 16166–16178, esp. 16169 (cf. Hertzberg, *l.c.*, p. 204) : —

"Par la ventaille le teneit."

"Aventayle" has been listed with "Romance words that end with a consonant in French [but] take an -e- in the *Troilus*," G. L. Kittredge, *Observations on the Language of Chaucer's Troilus*, p. 87; where the O. F. form "esventail" is given.   Broatch (*l.c.*, p. 19), who questions Skeat's attribution (*l.c.*, p. lx.) of the original to a passage in Guido, says, "Chaucer might perhaps be allowed to have invented the 'eventaille.'"   The aventaille of the twelfth to fourteenth centuries was a hood-shaped head-dress made of chain-mail, protecting the forehead and chin, on which the helmet rested, and the front part of which fell on the breast.   (J. Quicherat, *Mélanges d'archéologie*, etc., 1886, pp. 314–324; *Hist. du costume en France*, pp. 133, 288; Viollet-le-duc, *Dict. du mobilier français*, vol. VI. pp. 353–357; 105–107, Plates.)   Cf. Skeat, *Works of Chaucer*, vol. V. p. 352.

Lo here, the fyn and guerdon for travaille
Of Jove, Appollo, of Mars of swich rascaille
Lo here, the forme of olde clerkes speche.
In poetrye, if ye hir bokes seche,"[1]

which form a pendant to a preceding one
in which the *finale* of the story is given,
as found in the *Filostrato*,[2] he moralizes on
his poem,[3] showing an intolerance not found
elsewhere in his works[4] toward the pagan
deities, whom he has utilized for poetical

[1] *T. and C.*, V. 1849–1855; cf. V. 206–207, *B. of D.*
52–55 : —
> "And in this boke were written fables
> That clerkes hadde, in olde tyme
> And other poets, put in ryme
> To read."

[2] *T. and C.*, V. 1828–1834 = *Fil.*, VIII. 28.

[3] Cf. *L. of G. W.*, 468–474.

[4] There is only one other passage in Chaucer, and that
in a poem written in the same period as the *Troilus*, in
which a like sentiment is found. Cf. *The Former Age*,
57–59 : —
> "Yit was not Jupiter the likerous
> That first was father of delicacye,
> Come in this world,"

and with this cf. *Paradiso*, XV. 107 ff.

purposes in this very poem,[1] he shows the
influence of passages in the *Historia* in
which Guido inveighs against the deceptions
and falsities of heathendom.[2]

A Pandarus is mentioned first in the
list of allies who came to aid Troy, according to the narrative of both Benoit and
Guido, and the same person finds place in
another episode.[3]   Boccaccio has adopted

---

[1] *T. and C.*, I. 6–9; III. 1–46; IV. 22–26.

[2] *Historia*, sig. e 5 recto, col. 2 — e 6 recto, col. 1;
i 3 recto, col. 1.   In the *Troilus*, as in the other poems,
Chaucer shows an acquaintance with a late recension of
the *Roman de Thebes*.   For similarity in language and
sentiment with the stanza of Chaucer, these lines may be
quoted (*R. de T.* ed. Constans, col. II. p. 15, 4337–
4442) : —

> " Ffors solement danz Jupiter
>   Qui tint un dart agu de fer
>   Mars fu dejoste lui a destre;
>   Le proz Pallas fu a senestre
>   Cil dui valent en bataille;
>   Plus que toute l'autre raschaille."

[3] Among the combatants in the fourth battle is mentioned (*R. de T.* 11179) " Car le reis i fu Pandarus "

this name as that of the cousin of the heroine of the *Filostrato,* — who, in the *Troilus,* has become her uncle,[1] — and

(no equivalent in *Historia,* sig. h 4 verso, col. 1), who fights with Agamemnon (11217–11220) : —

> "Agamemnon et Pandarus
> Se porterent des chevax jus,
> Bien s'ateinstrent et se ferirent
> Et durement se combatirent,"

which Guido renders (*Historia,* sig. h 5 recto, col. 1), —

"Rex agamemnon et rex pandalus (*sic*) inter in simul concurrentes ambo se sternunt ab equis."

Lydgate (*Troy-book,* sig. Q i verso, col. 2) makes the name "Pantysylaus"; the *Gest Hystoriale,* 7460, omits the episode. There is nothing in the Latin text in the corresponding passages (*Historia,* sig. g 4 verso, col. 1; i 1 recto, col. 2) to answer to Benoit's mention (*R. de T.* 8101) of "Li reis Pandarus de Sezile," as one of those who did not go out to fight in the second battle ; nor to the lines, in the account of the conference of the Greeks and Trojans to arrange for the exchange of prisoners, and in which permission for the return of the daughter of Calchas to her father is granted (cf. p. 104), *R. de T.,* 12937–12939 : —

> "Agamemnon et Menelaus
> Reis Pandarus et Aïaus.
> Et li halt home des Grezeis."

[1] *Fil.,* II. 20, 6 ; 23, 2 ; 27, 7 = *T. and C.,* I. 975.

through his story, which passed through such various vicissitudes, in English it has come to be a term of reproach. Chaucer likewise has not hesitated to take a name from one of the sources, and by various changes, has created an entirely new character. In the list referred to, we find in Guido the phrase,—

"Sciendus est ergo quod de regnis eorum licet dares frigius nihil inde dixerit venerunt tres reges cum plus quam tribus milibus militum armatorum, rex videlicet Pandarus, rex Thabor et rex Andastrus,"[1]

[1] *Historia*, sig. f 5 verso, col. 1-2. "Pandorus" in text, but the correct reading is confirmed by the original passage in the *R de T.*, 6645–6646, cf. Constans, *l.c.*, p. 54:—

> " De Sezile i vint Pandarus
> Hupoz li vielz et Adrastus,"

(which in turn renders the phrase in Dares, 22, 15, "De Zelia Pandarus Amphius Adrastus"); and Lydgate's translation (*Troy-book*, sig. M 5 recto, col. 2), "The first of them was called Pandarus," although in the *Gest Hystoriale* (8536) he is given a Celtic surname — " Pen-

and just as the Italian writer made use of Pandarus, so Chaucer, by a metathesis of form and a change of sex, gives Criseyde

dragon the pert," while Adrastus becomes "Adasthon" (5438). Benoit based part of his episode of "the dread Saggitarius" (*R. de T.*, 12207–12348) upon the passage in Dictys (II. 40–41), which tells of the exploits of the Lycian archer, Pandarus, and his death by the hands of Diomedes. (Joly, *l.c.* vol. I. p. 209, cf. p. 229 ; W. Greif, *Die mittelalterichen Bearbeitungen der Troyanersage*, Marburg, 1885, p. 00.; R. Jaeckel, *Dares, Phrygius und Benoit de Ste. More*, Breslau, 1875, p. 53; E. Meybrinck, *l.c.*, p. 23.) This Pandarus and another, the companion of Æneas, are mentioned in the *Æneid* (V. 496; IX. 672; XI. 396). It is unnecessary to assume, as Hertzberg, that (*l.c.*, pp. 189–200, accepted by G. Koerting, *Boccaccio's Leben*, p. 591) " den Namen Pandarus als *vox hybrida* des Omens wegen ausgedeutet und fur den Freund gewählt hat, der dem Troilus alles giebt, Leben und Lebensglück." This explanation is based upon that given in a passage in the *Præmio* of the *Filostrato* in which the title is explained as being about a " uomo vinto e abbattuto da amore, (p. 1, cf. Hertzberg, *l.c.*, p. 197) ; but this symbolical explanation may not be Boccaccio's (cf. H. L. D. Ward, *Cat. of Romances*, vol. I. p. 68; P. Savj-Lopez, *Rom*, vol. XXVII. pp. 444–445). Landau, (*G. Boccaccio*, p. 90), and Morf (*Rom*, XXI. p. 106) notice the use of name in Benoit.

a niece with the name of Tharbe,[1] in the same way as he found the name of another niece, " Flexippe," in that of the uncle of Meleager, " Plexippus," [2] an outline of whose history is given in the *Troilus*,[3] taken from Ovid.[4]   Again, when Pandarus, to alarm Criseyde, states that Troilus —

[1] *T. and C.*, II. 815–816, 1563 : —

> " And up and doun ther made many a wente
> Flexippe, she, Tharbe and Antigone."

> " Antigone, hir sister Tarbe also."

[2] Ovid, *Met.*, VIII. 439–440 : —

> " hausitque nefando
> pectora Plexippi, nil tale timentia, ferro."

[3] *T. and C.*, V. 1464–1484; cf. *C.T.*, A, 2069–2071.

[4] Ovid, *Met.*, VIII. 260–532.   On Latin proper names of masculine gender which " have lost a final -*s*, sometimes with further change of form," cf. ten Brink, *Chaucers Sprache und Verskunst*, p. 264; Kittredge, *l.c.*, pp. 382–383, when the masculine form would be identical with the feminine as in this example.   The forms of the names in the line " Circes eke, and Calipsa " (*H. of F.*, 1272), are already found in Benoit and Guido.   Ulysses's adventures with Circe and Calypso in these two writers (*R. de T.*, 28576 ff., Constans in *Hist. de la langue et la leti. dt française*, p. 196; *Hist.*, sig. o 1 verso, col. 2;

> "seyth him told is, of a freend of his
How that ye sholde love oon that hatte Horaste,
For sorwe of which this night shall been his
>   laste,[1]

and the heroine denies the charge with the answer, —

> "Horaste ! allas ! and falsen Troilus ?
> I knewe him not, god helpe me so,"[2]

the name of this fictitious lover seems to have been borrowed from Guido's account of Orestes in which the name always appears as " Horestes."[3]

where false reading "Calipha "), form one episode, the source from which Gower drew his account, and to which he refers elsewhere. (*C. A.* VI. 1391 ff., VIII. 2598 ff. ; *Mirour de l'omme*, 16674 ff. ; *Balades*, XXX. 12 ; *Traitié*, VI. 17 ff.)

[1] *T. and C.*, III. 796–798.   [2] *Ibid.*, III. 806–807.

[3] *Historia*, sig. m 8 verso, col. 2 ; n 6 recto, col. 2, " De Horeste vindicante mortem patris," while in the *R. de T.* (27958, 28157, 28166, 28182) the name always appears as "Orestes." Kittredge (p. 347) notes the forms "Horestes," "Horest[e] " in Gower's account (*C. A.*, III. 1885 ff., cf. *Traitié* IX. 18), which is based upon both sources. The "fals Poliphete " (*T. and C.*, II. 1467, cf. 1615, 1618) who, in an episode which is

There are a number of details in the English poem, not found in the *Filostrato*, which could have been suggested equally

an innovation of the English poet (II. 1394–1757, III. 50–224), is charged by Pandarus with bringing "advocacyes newe" against Criseyde, must be the "Cererique sacrum Polyphoeten" of the *Æneid* (VI. 484) who as a Trojan priest could very properly take steps against the daughter of the renegade Calchas. The Greek leader Polypoetes, whom Hector is stripping of his armor, when he is slain by Achilles, according to the narrative of Dares (30, 5–10), does not appear in either Benoit or Guido. In that episode the name of the Greek is not given (*R. de T.*, 16166; *Historia*, sig. i 6 recto, col. 1), but the French poet, making two episodes of the one in his original, represents Hector as slaying one Politenes just before (*R. de T.*, 16105–16148; *Historia*, sig. i 5 verso, col. 2). This name is that substituted by Benoit (*R. de T.*, 5671, 8252–8253, "Politenes") for the classical Philoctetes (Dares, 19, 2), which again is displaced in Guido by Polipebus (*Historia*, sig. e 3 verso, col. 1), while Polypoetes appears in both authors as Polibetes (*R. de T.*, 5663, 8243, 9981; *Historia*, *l.c.*), and in Guido as a doublet of the name in the form Polipotes (*Historia*, *l.c.*). He appears elsewhere in Guido as Philotois (sig. g 4 verso, col. 2), and again as Philit(h)eas (sig. h 1 verso, col. 1; h 5 recto, col. 1), which corresponds in all these places to Benoit's *Filitoas* (*R. de T.*, 8189, 9065, 9375). T. E. Oliver, *Milet's Destruction de Troye.*, p. 229.

well by passages in either Benoit or Guido. Such are the allusions to the journey of Calchas to Delphi and his subsequent actions,[1] as he

" Knew wel that Troye sholde destroyed be,
    By answere, of his god, that highte thus,
    Daun Phebus or Apollo Delphicus.
    So whan this Calkas knew by calculinge
    And eek by answere of this Apollo,
    That Grekes sholden swich a peple bringe
    Thorugh which that Troye moste been
        for-do ; " [2]

" Appollo hath me told it feithfully ; " [3]

---

[1] Cf. p. 74, note.

[2] *T. and C.*, I. 68–74.   *Fil.*, I. 8, 7–8 has merely

  " Conobbe e vide, dopo lunga guerra
    I Troian morti e distrutta la terra,"

which is again translated in *T. and C.*, I. 76–77.

[3] *T. and C.*, IV. 114. Skeat (*l.c.*, p. 462) wrongly states that Guido puts Calchas " in the place of Homer's Chryses," as the latter appears in Benoit as a fellow-priest of the former (*R. de T.*, 25618–25619 ; *Historia*, sig. m 4 verso, col. 2), after he had come to the Greek camp to recover his daughter Astronomen (26746–26907), an incident omitted in *Historia*, sig. n 1 recto, col. 1.

" Thus shal I seyn, and that his coward herte
   Made him amis the goddes text to glose
   When he for ferde out of his Delphos sterte," [1]

and to the treason of Antenor, —

" This folk desiren now deliveraunce
   Of Antenor, that broughte hem to mischaunce!
   For he was after traytour to the toun
   Of Troye; allas! they quitte him out to
      rathe.
   O nyce world, lo, thy discrecioun! " [2]

which are told at length in both the Latin
and the French romances.[3]

Again, when Chaucer introduces Troilus
returning from battle past Criseyde's house:

" For thurgh this strete he moot to palays ryde;

   For other wey is fro the yate noon,
   Of Dardanus, there open is the cheyne," [4]

---

[1] *T. and C.*, IV. 1409–1411; cf. 1396, "For al Appollo, or his clerkes lawes."   [2] *T. and C.*, IV. 202–206.

[3] *R. de T.*, 24373–26038; *Historia*, sig. m 1 recto, col. 1; cf. Hertzberg, *l.c.*, p. 203; Skeat, *l.c.*, p. lvii; Broatch, *l.c.*, p. 16.

[4] *T. and C.*, II. 616–618. Skeat, *l.c.*, p. 470, thinks that the opening of the " cheyne " refers to the street.

there is a reminiscence of the passage in both authors, in which Hector orders that Dardanides, one of the six gates of Troy,[1] be opened to allow the egress of his army to meet the Greeks in their second battle.[2]

When Chaucer writes,—

" At whiche day was taken Antenore,
Maugre Polydamus or Monesteo,
Santippe, Sarpedon, Polynestore,
Polyte, or eek the Trojan daun Ripheo," [3]

he has been directly dependent upon Boccaccio for the list of names, even retaining their Italian forms,—

" Ed assai ve ne furon per prigioni
Nobili re, ed altri gran baroni.
Tra quali fu il magnifico Antenorre,
Polidamas suo figlio, e Monesteo,
Santippo, Serpedon, Polinestorre,
Polite ancora, ed il troian Rifeo," [4]

---

[1] *R. de T.*, 3129–3139; cf. Constans, *l.c.*, p. 67. *Historia*, sig. c 1 verso, col. 1; cf. Hertzberg, *l.c.*, pp. 191–192.

[2] *R. de T.*, 7643–7658; *Historia*, sig. g 3 recto, col. 2.

[3] *T. and C.*, IV. 50–53.   [4] *Fil.*, IV. 3, 1–4.

but has made a radical change in the statement of the facts. For both in the *Roman de Troie*[1] and the *Historia*,[2] Polydamas — the other names are additions of the Italian poet — appears, not as the fellow-prisoner, but as the distressed son who uselessly attempts the rescue of his father. And it was by this change that the English poet avoided the inconsistency of which Boccaccio was guilty in having Troilus and Pandarus visit Sarpedon, of whose return from captivity he makes no mention.[3]

Again, if Chaucer's lines, —

" Of Pryamus was yeve, at Greek request
  A tyme of trewe," [4]

---

[1] *R. de T.*, 12401–12415.

[2] *Historia*, sig. h 6 verso, col. 2 — i 1 recto, col. 1.

[3] *Fil.*, V. 38–48; *T. and C.*, V. 430–500; cf. W. M. Rossetti, *Comparison*, etc. p. 246; Skeat, *l. c.*, p. 497.

[4] *T. and C.*, IV. 57–58. Cf. variants : —

" But natheles a trewe was ther take
At gret requeste."

" To (of) Priamus was yeve at his (gret, Grek, Grekes) requeste
A time of trewe."

flatly contradict the statement in the *Filostrato*, —

" Chiese Priamo triegua, e fu gli data,"[1]

it is because the English poet accepted in preference the joint authority of his two other sources. According to Benoit and Guido, the Greeks send Ulysses and Diomedes as legates to ask for a cessation of hostilities under the plea that they wish to bury their dead, which are breeding disease in their camp. In the council that Priam calls, Hector alone speaks against granting the truce because he thinks that the true reason for the Greeks' request is that they may obtain provisions. But the opinion of the majority, with which Priam agrees, prevails,[2] and in an ensuing conference of the Trojan and Greek leaders, arrangements are made for the exchange of Thoas and

[1] *Fil.* IV. 4, 1.
[2] Cf. Dares, 27, 11–28, 3.

Antenor; and, at the request of Calchas through his superiors, Priam is not unwilling to allow the daughter of the recreant Trojan to go to her father in the Greek camp.[1]

And from this narrative Chaucer modified the story as he found it in his Italian prototype.   He follows Boccaccio in making the return of Antenor — who has been given to Calchas as a personal prisoner — contingent upon that of Criseyde,[2] but introduces Thoas, whom he does not elsewhere mention, as one of the parties in the exchange of prisoners : —

" And of this thing ful sone his nedes leyde
On hem that sholden for the tretis go,

---

[1] *R. de T.* 12690–12986; *Historia*, sig. i 1 recto, col. 1; i 1 verso, col. 1; cf. wrong account in Skeat. *l.c.*, p. 486.

[2] *Fil.*, IV. 10, 4–6; 12, 7–8; 13; 14, 1–3; 15, 6–8; 17, 5–8; 43, 1–4; 78, 7–8; VI, 19, 2–3; *T. and C.*, IV. 111, 133–136, 140–147, 149, 177, 195–196, 207–212, 344–347, 663–665; V. 905.   There is no equivalent in the English poem for *Fil.*, V. 1, 2–3; 8, 5–8.   Cf. Oliver, *Milet's Destruction*, pp. 98–100.

And hem for Antenor ful ofte preyde
To bringen hoom king Thoas [1] and Criseyde." [2]

Again, the speech of Hector in the Trojan
" parlement" against the exchange of a
woman for a man,[3] which finds no precedent
in the *Filostrato*, was no doubt suggested
by the similar position he takes concerning the truce in the common sources of the
English and Italian poems, and the outcry
of the people against this plea [4] is suggestive

[1] The manuscript reading " Toas," adopted by Skeat,
is not justified by spelling in either Benoit or Guido.

[2] *T. and C.*, IV. 135–138; cf. Hertzberg. *l.c.*, p. 203.
Lydgate *Troy-book*, sig. Q 5 verso, col. 2, r verso,
col. 2 ff., has combined the narratives of Guido and
Chaucer. It may be noted that MS. Harl., 1239, an in-
ferior manuscript, has a reading which obviates the
" Thoas " episode in Chaucer : —

> " And hem ful ofte specyally preyde
> For Antenor to bringe home Creseide "

(Globe *Chaucer*, p. 510; cf. p. xlii.; Skeat, *l.c.*, lxxii.).

[3] *T. and C.*, IV. 176–182; cf. Chaucer's introduction
of him as a friend of Criseyde in her case against Poliphete, II. 1450–1466, 1481; cf. I, 113–123.

[4] *T. and C.*, IV. 183–196.

of their better expression of opinion upon
Calchas when they learn that he wishes his
daughter, as stated in the same authorities.[1]

When the heroine meets her father, she

" Stood forth mewet, milde, and mansuete,"[2]

as in the *Filostrato,*

" Ella si stava tacita e modesta," [3]

while in the narrative of both their predecessors, the heroine reproaches her father
bitterly for having such faith in the answers
of Apollo, which are not assured, as to leave
his honorable position in Troy to become an
ally of the bitter foes of his native country; [4]
to which Calchas replies by saying, that he
has the undoubted promise of the gods that
Troy will be destroyed in a short time, and
that it will be better for them to escape the
fate of the other inhabitants; whereupon
Breseida seems to accept the situation, espe-

---

[1] *R. de T.,* 12967–12972; *Historia,* sig. i 1 verso, col. 1.
[2] *T. and C.,* V. 194.   [3] *Fil.,* V. 14, 3.
[4] Broatch (*l.c.,* p. 16) says that in Guido, " the speech
of Briseida is mere railing."

cially when the Greek princes receive her with all kindness.[1] But just as Boccaccio in the discussion of Troilus with his mistress before her departure from Troy anticipates the speech of Calchas,[2] and foretells her favorable reception by the Greeks,[3] so Chaucer in the corresponding place in his poem has Criseyde tell how she is going to rebuke her father.[4]

In Boccaccio's poem, the heroine merely states that she will persuade her father to allow her return to Troy, to recover her property which

" el per avarizia
Della mia ritornata avrà letizia." [5]

[1] *R. de T.*, 13684–13830; *Historia*, sig. i 2 verso, col. 2 — i 3 recto, col. 2.

[2] *Fil.*, IV. 142, 2–3; *T. and C.*, IV. 1479–1482; cf. *R. de T.*, 13767–13778. *Historia*, sig. i 3 recto, col. 1, " Scio enim . . . trucidatis."

[3] *Fil.*, IV. 142, 4–5; *T. and C.*, IV. 1485–1488; *R. de T.*, 13814–13822. *Historia*, sig. i 3 recto, cols. 1–2, " In adventu . . . replent eam."

[4] Cf. Skeat, *l.c.*, p. lvii.; Broatch, *l.c.*, p. 16.

[5] *Fil.*, IV. 136.

In the *Troilus* this is elaborated into a
definite plan, by which she is to bribe,
deceive, and cajole Calchas into repudiat-
ing the authority of the oracles of Apollo.[1]
And, in the following lines, there is a
reminiscence of the speech of Brisaide to
her father in the earlier writers: —

[1] *T. and C.*, IV. 1356–1414. Cf. "Amphibologia;
ambigua dictio . . . ut illud responsum Apollinis ad
Pyrrhum,

'Aio te, Aiacida, Romanos vincere posse.'

In quo non est certum quem in ipso versu monstraverit
esse victorem" (Isidorus, *Etymologiarum*, Lib. I. ch. 34;
Migne, *Patr.*, vol. 82, col. 109).   Chaucer makes use of another etymology from the same source in the *Persones
Tale*, where "seint Isidre" is referred to at first hand (*C.
T.*, I. 551; *Etym.*, Lib. XVII. ch. 7; Migne, *l.c.*, col. 615;
cf. *C. T.*, I. 85).   But the first definition of Isidore is
based upon a chapter in Cicero's *De Divinatione* (II. 56),
where oracles are scored in a passage much resembling
Chaucer's lines, "Tuis enim oraculis Chrysippus totum
volumen implevit partim falsis, ut ego opinor, partim casu
veris, ut fit in omni oratione sæpissime, partim flexiloquis
et obscuris ut interpres egeat interprete et *sors* ipsa ad
sortes referenda sit, partim ambiguis, et quæ ad dialec-
tum deferendæ sint."   Then follow references to "hanc
amphiboliam" (in inferior texts "amphibologiam"),

" For al Appollo, or his clerkes lawes,
Or calculinge avayleth nought three hawes;

the answer of the oracle to Pyrrhus, cited above, and
" illa amphibolia," which was given to Crœsus.

Chaucer's definition of Boccaccio's word " ambages "
(*T. and C.*, V. 898–899), —

" That is to seyn, with double wordes slye,
Swich as men clepe a word 'with two visages,' "

is rather that of " amphibologyes," which he uses as a
synonym. A misunderstanding of another passage (*De
Div.*, II. 54–55, " Quamobrem . . . Cassandra ") seemed
to have supplied him with his second name for Cassandra (*T. and C.*, V. 1450–1451) : —

" For which he for Sibille his suster sente
That called was Cassandre eek al aboute."

This work of Cicero is largely taken up with an
adverse criticism of the work of the Stoic Chrysippus on
dreams and oracles, and it may be to it that Chaucer
refers, in the *Wife of Bath's Prologue*, as being one of
the books " bounden in one volume " that Jankin had
(*C. T.*, D, 677) : —

" Crisippus, Trotula, and Helowys."

Chaucer had found the *De Divinatione* cited in Boethius (B. V. pr. 4, 11, 3 ff.), and made use of it at first
hand in the *Nonne Preestes Tale* (*C. T.*, B, 4174–4294;
De Div., I. 27. Cf. *C. T.*, B, 4113–4126; *T. and C.*, V.
369–371; *De Div.*, I. 29. Cf. K. O. Petersen, *Sources of
Nonne Preestes Tale*, pp. 106–110). Cf. *Works of Chaucer*,
vol. V., p. 309.

Desyr of gold shal so his sowle blende
That, as me lyst, I shal wel make an ende.

" And if he wolde ought by his sort it preve
If that I lye, in certayn I shal fonde
Distorben him, and plukke him by the sleve,
Makinge his sort, and beren him on honde,
He hath not wel the goddes understonde.
For goddes speken in amphibologyes,
And, for a sooth, they tellen twenty lyes.

" Eek drede fond first goddes, I suppose,
Thus shal I seyn, and that his coward herte,
Made him amis the goddes text to glose,
Whan he for ferde out of his Delphos sterte." [1]

Again, when Troilus foresees the arguments of her father against her return to the city, —

---

[1] *T. and C.*, IV. 1397–1411.   Cf. *R. de T.*, 13732–13737; *Historia*, sig. i 3 recto, col. 1: —

  "Sane deceperunt te Apollinis falsa responsa "

(cf. *Fil.*, VII. 90, 7–8),

  " Sane non fuit ille deus Appollo sed potius puto fuit comitiva infernalium furiarum a quibus responsa suscepisti."

Cf. Skeat (*l.c.* p. lvii); Broatch (*l.c.*, p. 16); also p. 99.

" And over al this, your fader shal despyse
  Us alle, and seyn this citee nis but lorn ;
  And that th' assege never shal aryse,
  For-why the Grekes han it alle sworn
  Til we be slayn, and doun our walles torn," [1]

he has enlarged upon two lines of the
Filostrato,[2] by borrowing from his other
sources.[3] Chaucer's comment upon Criseyde's promises to use every means to
return to Troy, —

[1] *T. and C.*, IV. 1478–1482.   [2] Cf. p. 74, n.

[3] *R. de T.*, 13767–13773. Cf. A. Mussafia, *Sitzb. der
Wiener Ak. Phil.-Hist. Klasse*, vol. 67, p. 324 : —

    " Ensorquetot bien vei et sei,
      Que morz et destruiz les verrai
      Si nos vient mielz aillors garir
      Que la dedanz o els morir.
      Mort seront il, vencu et pris ;
      Car li Deu l'ont issi permis,
      Ce ne puet mès longues durer ; "

Historia, sig. i 3 recto, col. 1 : —

    " Scio enim pro certo per infabilium promisa deorum
presentem guerram protendi non posse tempore diuturno
et quod civitas Troie brevi tempore destruatur et ruat,
destructis ejus omnibus nobilibus et universis plebeis ejus
in ore gladii trucidatis. Quare carissima filia, satis est
melius nobis hic esse quam hostili gladio serviente perire."
Cf. p. 107, note 2.

" And treweliche, as writen wel I finde,
 That al this thing was seyd of good entente,
 And that hir herte trewe was and kinde
 Towardes him, and spak right as she mente,
 And that she starf for no neigh, whan she
   wente
 And was in purpos ever to be trewe,
 Thus writen they that of hir werkes knewe," [1]

part of which he restates later on, —

" And trewely, as men in bokes rede,
 Men wiste never womman han the care,
 Ne was so looth out of a toun to fare," [2]

has no parallel in the *Filostrato*, and reverses
the sentiments of Benoit and Guido, as the
first comments on the fickle nature of the
heroine,[3] while the latter follows up his
account of Brisaide's sorrow at parting by
slurs upon her sincerity, and a diatribe
against the faithlessness of woman.[4]

---

[1] *T. and C.*, IV. 1415–1421.   [2] *Ibid.*, V. 19–21.
[3] *R. de T.* 13403–13408, 13826–13827.
[4] *Historia*, sig. i 2 recto, col. 2.   *T. and C.*, IV. 1695–
1701, is not suggested by any passage in either Benoit or
Guido (Skeat, *l.c.*, p. lvii.; Broatch, *l.c.*, p. 17).   Chaucer

The declaration of his passion to Criseyde by Diomedes[1] and her answer in their ride to her father's tent[2] after Troilus has delivered her into his care,[3] has its precedent in both the O. F. and Latin romances, although Chaucer is directly

has merely developed one stanza of the *Filostrato* (IV. 167) into two of his own (1688–1701). "The day gan ryse" translates the Italian "s'appressava Gia l'aurora," which seems in turn to be suggested by Guido's phrase, "Sed diei hora quasi superveniente," (*Historia*, sig. i 2 recto, col. 1).

[1] Cf. *T. and C.*, V. 88, "The sone of Tydeus" with *R. de T.*, 13499, "Filz Tideus." Cf. p. 115, n. 2.

[2] *T. and C.*, V. 92–175.

[3] Cf. *Fil.*, V. 12, 2–3 : —

"a Diomede Non parlò punto,"

with *T. and C.*, V. 86–87 : —

"and unto Diomede
No word he spak, ne noon of all his route,"

where, in Chaucer's addition, may be a reminiscence of the list of distinguished Greeks who accompanied Diomedes, according to the narrative in the *R. de T.*, 13490–13494, for which Guido (*Historia*, sig. i 2 verso, col. 1) has merely, "Sed Grecis advenientibus ad recipiendum eandem." Cf. Oliver, *l.c.*, p. 100.

I

dependent upon the speech of the Greek
lover in the *Roman de Troie*,[1] and not
upon the mere summary of the same in
Guido's work,[2] although he has abridged
Criseyde's answer, not from that found in
Benoit,[3] but from the one given by the

---

[1] *R. de T.*, 13502, 13589, 13649–13673. Cf. particularly
R. de T., 13499, 13574–13580, 13526–13528, 13561–13566,
13523–13525, 13543–13551, with *T. and C.*, V. 88, 109–
112, 155–158, 162–165, 169–175; and with the last cf.
the speech of Troilus where same passage has been used,
T. and C., IV. 1485–1488. The same passage of Benoit
has been utilized in the *Fil.*, VI. 14–25, VI. 21 = *T. and
C.*, V. 1489–1490. Chaucer, making the first step in Diomedes' wooing in Boccaccio's poem the second in his
own, translates this in *T. and C.* (V. 855–942, but 940
not in *Fil.* Cf. *T. and C.*, V. 155–157).

[2] *Historia*, sig. i 2 verso, col. 1.

[3] *R. de T.*, 13585–13643.   Yet Chaucer says (V. 176)
that she "lyte answerde" Broatch (*l.c.*, p. 17; cf. 18, 27);
"But Benoit has, 13671, the original of the Chaucerian
'thanked Diomede.'"   The *R. de T.*, 13671–13672, does
state that Diomedes: —

> " Li a cri cent feiz merci
>   Que de lui face son ami."

(Cf. *R de T.*, 14985, with *T. and C.*, V. 1011) ; which is
not quite the same thing.

latter's plagiarist.[1]   The description of Diomedes, —

"This Diomedes as bokes us declare,
    Was in his nedes prest and corageous;
    With sterne voys and mighty limes square,
    Hardy, testif, strong and chevalrous
    Of dedes, lyk his father Tideus,
    And son men seyn, he was of tunge large,
    And heir he was of Calidoine and Arge,"[2]

is an enlargement upon the lines of the
Filostrato, —

[1] Cf. p. 83; Hertzberg, *l.c.*, p. 203; Skeat, *l.c.*, p. lvii.;
Broatch, *l.c.*, p. 17.

[2] *T. and C.*, V. 799–805.   Cf. 803–805, with *T. and C.*,
V. 932–934 : —

    "'For if my fader Tydeus,' he seyde,
        'Y-lived hadde, I hadde been er this,
        Of Calidoine and Arge a king, Criseyde!'"
= *Fil.* VI. 24, 1, 3 : —

        "Se 'l padre mio Tideo fosse vissuto,
            Di Calidonia et d' Argo saria suto."

Guido's statement (*Historia*, sig. 3 verso, col. 1), "diomedes ... de terra sua argis," has been enlarged upon by
Lydgate, unquestionably upon the authority of Chaucer,
into "fro Calidonye and Arge" (*Troy-book*, sig. R 4
verso, col. 1).   Cf. Skeat's confused statement on the
matter (*l.c.*, p. 490).

" Egli era grande e bel della persona
　Giovane fresco e piacevole assai,
　E forte e fier siccome si ragiona,
　E parlante quant' altro Greco mai," [1]

by hints drawn from Chaucer's other
authorities.　The lines in Benoit's description of Diomedes, —

" Groz et *quarrez* et granz adès," [2]

" Molt par fu *hardiz* et veisos," [3]

---

[1] *Fil.*, VI. 33, 1–4 ; cf. with *l.* 4, *R. de T.*, 5198–5199 : —

" Mès de parole esteit noisos
E molt esteit fox sorparlez,"

and quotation from Guido on p. 118.　On defective lines
in *T. and C.*, V. 799–840, W. S. McCormick, *l.c.*, p. 543.

[2] *R. de T.*, 5194.　But Chaucer may have gone back
to Benoit's original, which offers a closer analogue to his
own expression, "quadratum corpore" (Dares, 16, 19–
20), which, however, may be better compared with the
phrase in the description of Ajax, "quadratum valentibus
membris" (Dares, 16, 14–15), which Benoit renders
(*R. de T.*, 5161–5162) : —

" Aiaus fu gros et quarrez
De piz, de braz et de costez."

Cf. Skeat, *l.c.*, p. lviii. ; Broatch, *l.c.*, pp. 17, 26–27.

[3] *R. de T.*, 5197.

show at once the source of two of the
details in the English poem.   In another
passage in the *Roman de Troie*, Achilles
thus characterizes Diomedes in addressing
him, —

> " Sire, gie ne me merveil mie
>   Se vos amez chevalerie
>   Si fetes vos, ne poez plus
>   Mar fussiez vos filz Tidéus.
>   Se par vos n'ert toustans meintenue ; " [1]

> " Or estes garni et prest
>   De fere autretel," [2]

and the hints borrowed thence by Chaucer are too apparent to further specify.
The term " testif " would state in a word

[1] *R. de T.*, 19747–19751 *ed.* " chevalelie," " n'est bien
meintenue"; but cf. L. Constans, *Roman de Thebes*, vol.
II. p. cxvi. 2.

[2] *R. de T.*, 19764–19765.   This passage is in the
account of the embassy of Ulysses, Nestor, and Diomedes
to persuade Achilles, who refrains from the war on
account of his love for Polyxena, to come to the aid of
the Greeks in their distress, but their prayers and reproaches are in vain.   Guido's account is very much
abridged (*R. de T.*, 19395–19779; *Historia*, sig. k 5

Guido's description of an unpleasant feature in the personality of the Greek hero : —

" servientium sibi nimis impatiens cum molestus servientibus nimis esset."[1]

The visit of Diomedes to the tent of Calchas to woo Criseyde is found only in the *Filostrato,* but his action at parting, —

" And after this, the sothe for to seyn,
Hir glove he took of which he was ful fayn,"[2]

is transposed from its proper place in Chaucer's two other sources, where the same incident occurs, when Diomedes leaves the heroine at her father's camp.[3] And it is to the lines of Benoit, —

verso, col. 2 to k. 6 recto col. 2).   Cf. " in his nedes," with *T. and C.,* III. 1772.   " In alle nedes " = *Fil.* III. 90, 1, " Nell'opere opportune."

[1] *Historia,* sig. e 2 recto, col. 1; cf. Dares, 16, 20, "impatientem."   For the detail "with sterne voys," there is no equivalent in either the French or Latin texts, but the same characterization may have been applied to a different feature.   Cf. *R. de T.,* 5195, "La chière avoit molt felonesse."   *Historia, l.c.,* "aspectu ferox."

[2] *T. and C.,* V. 1012–1013.   [3] Cf. p. 113.

" Un de ses ganz li a toleit
Que nus nel seit ne perceit
Molt s'en fait liez," [1]

rather than to Guido's paraphrase, —

" unam de cirothecis quam Brisaida gerebat in manu ab ea nullo percipiente furtive subtraxit," [2]

that this touch is due.   Again, when Chaucer writes, —

" And after this the story telleth us
That she him yaf the faire baye stede,
The which she ones wan of Troilus," [3]

he makes statements of facts, for which

[1] *R. de T.*, 13673–13675.

[2] *Historia*, sig. i 2 verso, col. 2; cf. Skeat, *l.c.*, pp. lix., 499; Broatch, *l.c.*, p. 18.   Yet in the phrase which directly precedes, there is perhaps the hint — not found in Benoit — for a couple of lines of Chaucer : —

"Quare associavit eam usque ad locum quo Bresaida recipere in sui patris tentoria se debebat, et ea perveniente ibidem ipse eam ab equo descendens promptus adivit."

Cf. *T. and C.*, V. 181–182, 189 : —

" For wan she gan hir fader for aspeye,
Wel neigh doun of hir hors she gan to sye."

" And from her hors she alighte."

[3] *T. and C.*, V. 1037–1039.   In 1039, I accept Thynne's reading "she" in preference to "he" of all the manu-

Benoit was the sole authority;[1] and if in the following lines, —

" And eek a broche (and that was litel nede)
    That Troilus was, she yaf this Diomede,"[2]

scripts (cf. Skeat, *l.c.* pp. 499, lxxiii.), as it accords with a statement in Benoit's account of his heroine's loan of the horse to Diomedes (*R. de T.*, 15009–15014) : —

> " Un jor iert alé préier
>   Qu'ele remirot le destrier
>   Qui Troylus avoit esté
>   L'en li ot bien dit et conté
>   Qu'a sa mie en esteit presenz
>   Iriez en iert et molt dolenz."

Cf. *Works of Chaucer*, ed. Bell, vol. VI. p. 23. Reading " he," the line would allude to another passage in the O.F. poem, which was rendered in Guido's work, recounting the capture of the horse of Troilus, by Diomedes, who had unseated its rider, and its presentation to the heroine, — an act of courtesy often mentioned in romances, *R. de T.*, 14238–14303; cf. L. Constans, *Les MSS. du Roman de Troie*, in *Études romanes dediées a G. Paris*, p. 214; *Historia*, sig. i 4 recto, col. 1; cf. *Buev. de Com.*, 2661 ff.; *R. de Thebes*, 4363 ff.; *Saisnes*, vol. I. pp. 122, 126; *Perceval*, 6887 ff.; *Fergus*, 4972 ff.

[1] *R. de T.*, 15009–15054; cf. Skeat, *l.c.*, pp. 499, lxxx.; Broatch, *l.c.*, pp. 18–19, 25.

[2] *T. and C.*, V. 1040–1041; cf. Skeat (*l.c.*, p. 503), who does not find incident in Guido.

he adopts Boccaccio's setting of the same incident, in the *Filostrato*,[1] it was to the O.F. poem that he had to have recourse[2] when he continues with : —

[1] *Fil.*, VIII. 8, 9–10 ; *T. and C.*, V. 1658–1678 ; cf. *T. and C.*, III. 1370–1372 : —

"But wel I woot a broche, gold and asure,
   In whiche a ruby set was lyk an herte,
   Criseyde him yaf, and stak it on his sherte,"

where Chaucer introduces a new detail in his story, by attributing to Criseyde an action at an early period in her connection with Troilus, which, following Boccaccio, he has attributed to the hero at the time of their parting. Again, Chaucer had no precedent in any of his sources when he attributes to the lovers a common custom (*T. and C.*, III. 1368–1369 ; cf. P. Meyer ; Girart de Roussillon, p. 18, n. 1 ; Godefroi de Bouillon, 15, 553), —

"And pleyinge entrechaungeden hir ringes
   Of which I can nought tellen no scripture,"

or when Criseyde says to Pandarus (*T. and C.*, III. 885) : —

"Have here, and bereth him this blewe ring."

[2] *R. de T.*, 15102–15104. Seeing this on the lance of Diomedes (15576–15577), Troilus may know that he is forgotten by his beloved (15109–15112) ; furnishing the

" And eek, the bet from sorwe him to releve,
    She made him were a pencel of hir sleve." [1]

And while there is reference to more than
one authority in the lines, —

"I finde eek in the stories elles-where,
    Whan *through the body* hurt was Diomede
    Of Troilus, tho weep she many a tere,
    Whan that she saugh his wyde woundes blede;
    And that she took to kepen him good hede," [2]

there are details mentioned which are only
found in the French romance. Thus Guido's
phrase, —

"ipsum (*i.e.* Diomedes) precipitem dejecit ab
equo et mortaliter vulneravit," [3]

same motive as is supplied by the brooch in Boccaccio
which Chaucer made use of. (Cf. note, p. 121, n. 1). For
custom, cf. *R. de Thebes*, 4455, 8963; *R. d'Alexandre*, 401,
7; *Enéas*, 9331: *Octavian*, 2694, 3405; *Anseis*, 2002, 3634,
4719, 5000; *Rom*, vol. IV. p. 30; *Jahr. f. rom. u. engl.
Lit.*, vol. IX. p. 34; *Auberi*, 74, 18; 78, 13; *Perceval*, 6866.

    [1] *T. and C.*, V. 1042–1043; cf. Skeat., *l.c.*, pp. 499,
lxxx.; Broatch, *l.c.*, p. 24.

    [2] *T. and C.*, V. 1044–1048.

    [3] *Historia*, sig. k 6 verso, col. 2.

omits the specific statement found in the passage of the *Roman de Troie*, of which Chaucer has made use in the above lines, —

> "Come il navra Diomedes
>   *Parmi le cors* de plein eslès,"[1]

just as in Troilus's vow that if he meets his successful rival, —

> "trewely, if I have might and space
> Yet shall I make, I hope, *his sydes blede*,"[2]

there is a reminiscence of the fuller description elsewhere in Benoit: —

> "Ala ferir Diomedes
>   D'une lance grosse et poignal
>   Si que l'enseigne de cendal
>   Li remest *parmi les costez*."[3]

Nor is there a suggestion in the Latin of the French lines, —

> "Mès n'en puet pas son cuer covrir
>   Que plor, e lermes, et sospir

[1] *R. de T.*, 545–546; cf. Broatch, *l.c.*, p. 25.
[2] *T. and C.*, V. 1704–1705.   [3] *R. de T.*, 20066–20069.

N'issent de li a negun fuer

.   .   .   .   .   .

E ele en plore o les deus ièlz," [1]

as there is in the English poem.

And, again, the reason of the change of number to the singular is apparent when Chaucer writes, —

> " But trewely the story telleth us,
>   Ther made never womman more wo
>   Than she, whan that she falsed Troilus," [2]

as the soliloquy which follows is a somewhat close version of a passage in the *Roman de Troie*,[3] of which Guido has only

---

[1] *R. de T.*, 20197–20199, 20213.   On form *ielz, ueuz,* cf. Constans., *l.c.*, p. 47; *Ét ded. a G. Paris*, p. 224, n.

[2] *T. and C.*, V. 1051–1053.

[3] *R. de T.*, 20227–20330; *T. and C.*, V. 1054–1085; cf. esp. *R. de T.*, 20228–20229, 20233–20234 (cf. 20255), 20245–20252 (cf. 20665–20669), 20265–20268 (cf. 20310, 20317–20329), 20269–20274, 20308, 20277–20280, 20234; *T. and C.*, 1058–1060, 1056–1057, 1061–1066, 1068–1071, 1072–1074, 1026–1027, 1734.   Cf. Hertzberg, *l.c.*, p. 204, Skeat, *l.c.*, p. 500; Broatch, *l.c.*, p. 24.

a short summary,[1] and which was entirely omitted by Boccaccio.

If the English poet, after telling of her final decision to return the love of Diomedes, declares, —

" Ne me ne list this sely womman chyde
    Ferther than the story wol devyse.
    Hir name, allas ! is publisshed so wyde,
    That for hir gilt it oughte y-now suffyse.
    And if I mighte excuse hir any wyse,
    For she so sorry was for hir untrouthe,
    Y-wis, I wolde excuse hir yet for routhe,"[2]

as in an earlier passage he writes, —

" For how Criseyde Troilus forsook,
    Or at the leste, how that she was unkinde,
    Mot hennes-forth ben matere of my book,
    As wryten folk thorugh which it is in minde.
    Allas ! that they shulde ever cause finde
    To speke hir harm ; and if they on hir lye,
    Y-wis, hemself sholde han the vilanye,"[3]

---

[1] *Historia*, sig. l 1 recto, col. 1.
[2] *T. and C.*, V. 1093–1099.   [3] *Ibid.*, IV. 15–21.

in the first of these passages there is a veiled allusion, as in the second a direct reference, to the slighting comments of Guido upon the actions of the heroine in particular,[1] as well as upon the falsity of womankind in general, which in his character of a woman-hater he brings in throughout his work.

While, in the *Filostrato*,[2] Cassandra, who has heard from Deiphobus the cause of the evil plight of Troilus which he had accidentally discovered, comes to persuade the latter to forget the faithless low-born daughter of Calchas, in the *Troilus*[3] the hero sends for her as a seer to interpret his dream, — to which in the Italian poem

---

[1] *Historia*, sig. i 2 recto, col. 2; i 3 recto, col. 2; l 1 recto, col 1; yet for the general statements Guido found his material in the *R. de T.* (cf. 13412–13465, 14968–14982). Lydgate bitterly reproaches Guido for his misogyny = *Troy-book*, sig. d 1 verso, col. 2; Hertzberg, *l.c.*, 185; Dunger, *l.c.*, p. 62, n.   Morf., *Rom*, vol. XXI. p. 92.

[2] *Fil.*, VII. 77–87.   [3] *T. and C.*, V. 1443–1526.

he himself has given the same meaning,[1] —
and in introducing this new motive, Chaucer has been unquestionably influenced by
the prominent part which this daughter of
Priam's plays in the mediæval Troy legend,
and from which, as it has been noticed,
he took the cue in other poems.[2] Chaucer's
indebtedness for different details in his few
lines upon Hector's death, to both his
French and Latin sources, has already been
noted.   And again, in the lines that tell of
the grief which it caused, —

" For whom, as olde bokes tellen us
  Was maad swich wo, that tonge it may not telle,
  And namely, the sorwe of Troilus,"[3]

it is to be noticed that he has supplemented
Boccaccio's general statement, —

[1] *Fil.*, VII. 27; *T. and C.*, V. 1513–1519. It may be noted
that, as in the *Filostrato* (VII. 88), Troilus supposes that
his sister gained her knowledge through divination, his
reproach of her incompetence (VII. 89–90) is made use
of by Chaucer (*T. and C.*, V. 1520–1529).

[2] Cf. pp. 62–63.   [3] *T. and C.*, V. 1562–1564.

" L' alto dolor, da non poter mai dire,[1]
Che 'l padre, ed egli e' fratei per la morte
Ebber d' Ettor,"[2]

by a specific detail of which the source is
in Benoit's lines, —

" Molt le regrete Troylus
Car riens soz ciel n'amot il plus." [3]

Again, the lines, —

" In many cruel batayle, out of drede,
Of Troilus, this ilke noble knight,
As men may in these olde bokes rede,
Was sene his knighthod and his grete might.

[1] Cf. *R. de T.*, 16305–16307 : —

" Là est li dols si angoisseos
Si pesmes et si dolereos
Que nel porreit riens raconter."

Gest Historale, 8717 : —

" Hit were tore any tunge tell hit with mouthe."

[2] *Fil.*, VIII. 1, 3–5.

[3] *R. de T.*, 16351–16352. The grief of Paris is there,
however, " namely " set forth, 16323–16350. Guido merely
has (*Historia*, sig. i 6 recto, col. 2) : —

Sic et dolentes fratres ejusdem dolores casu universa-
liter torquebantur.

And dredelees, his ire, day and night,
Ful cruelly the Grekes ay aboughte," [1]

for which the *Filostrato* only offers a single parallel line, —

" Nelle battaglie Troilo sempre entrava," [2]

allude to the combats in which Troilus was preëminent after the death of Hector, which are fully described by both Benoit [3] and Guido. [4]

---

[1] *T. and C.*, V. 1751–1756. On phrase "his ire aboughte" cf., pp. 66, n. 2, and *Fil.*, VIII, 27, 1–2 = *T. and C.*, V. 1800–1801 : —

> "L' ira di Troilo in tempi diversi
> A Greci nocque molto senza fallo."

[2] *Fil.*, VIII. 25, 7.

[3] *R. de T.*, 19153–19174, 19350–19355, 19994–20021, 20123–20139, 20454–20464, 20529–20534, 20560–20564, 20820–20828, 21174–21175.

[4] *Historia*, sig. k 5 verso, col. 1–l 2 verso, col. 2; Guido's phrase (*Historia*, sig. i 5 verso, col. 1), in the account of the combat in which Troilus and Diomedes would have killed each other if Menelaus had not interfered, —

"se graviter impetunt in duris ictibus lancearum,"
is nearer Chaucer's "Assayinge how hir speres weren whette" (*T. and C.*, V. 1760), than Boccaccio's, —

K

Chaucer's account of Troilus's death is summed up in one line, —

"Dispitously him slough the fiers Achille,"[1]

> "E di gran colpi fra lor si donaro,
> Talvolta, urtando e talor nelle mani
> Le spade avendo " (*Fil.* VIII. 26, 3–5),

which seems to have its source in the *R. de T.*, 15588–15591, —

> "A ferir d'espée et de lance
> Tel geu voleient comencier
> O les clers trenchanz branz d'acier
> De quei les testes lor seignassent,"

of which the last line seems to suggest Chaucer's (*T. and C.*, V. 1762) lines : —

> "And god it woot, with many a cruel hete,
> Gan Troilus upon his helm to bete."

Chaucer's line, *T. and C.*, V. 1802, "For thousandes his hondes maden deye" is a modification of Boccaccio's (*Fil.*, VIII. 28, 7) "Avendone gia morti più di mille," for which Guido (*Historia*, sig. k 6 verso, col. 1), "Scripsit enim Dares quod illo die mille milites interfecit ex Grecis," gave the information. Cf. Dares, ed. Meister, p. xlvi. The same feat is attributed to Hector, *R. de T.*, 9957–9958; *Historia*, sig. i 4 recto, col. 1. Cf. Skeat, *l.c.*, p. lx.; Broatch, *l.c.*, pp. 19–20.

[1] *T. and C.*, V. 1806.

a translation of his Italian original, —

"Miseramente un dì l' uccise Achille,"[1]

but there is a suggestion of the manner of his death in an imprecation, not found in the *Filostrato*,[2] which the hero calls down on himself, if he should ever be ungrateful to Pandarus for his services : —

"And, if I lye, Achilles with his spere
    Myn herte cleve."[3]

Now in the narrative of both Benoit[4] and Guido,[5] Achilles is represented as slaying Troilus by cutting off his head, but, in one version of a Middle English summary of a part of the *Roman de Troie*, there is evidence collateral with that given in Chaucer, of the tradition according to which Achilles pierces his Trojan opponent with a spear — a point brought out in the *Troilus* of

---

[1] *Fil.*, VIII. 27, 8.   [2] *Fil.*, III. 15.
[3] *T. and C.*, III. 374–375.
[4] *R. de T.*, 21415–21416.
[5] *Historia*, sig. 1 2 verso, col. 2.

Sophocles,[1] and in vase paintings which departed from the more common version to follow that of the Greek tragedian.[2]   In the *Seege of Troye*, as' it appears in MS. Harl. 525, it is stated that Achilles, after a long fight with swords,

> " Smote Sir Troyell to þe herte
> Even ato his body he deled."[3]

If the first of these lines is anything more than a mere conventional phrase, its coincidence with Chaucer's statement is striking; but only after the publication of

[1] Schol., *in Iliad*, XXIV. 257, as amended by F. G. Welcker, *Zeit. f. Alterthumsw.*, 1834, No. 3, p. 30; *Die griechischen Tragödien mit Rücksicht auf den epischen Cyclus.*, 1839, vol. I. p. 124; Eustathius, *in Il.*, XXIV. 257. Cf. W. Klein, *Euphronios*, 1878, p. 77, n. 2.

[2] Welcker, *l.c.*, vol. I. pp. 124–129; J. Overbeck, *Die Bildwerke zum thebischen und troischen Heldenkreis.* 1853, p. 338; Klein, *l.c.*, p. 85; Zuckenbach, in *Jahns Jahr. Suppl.*, vol. XI. pp. 610–612; cf. 603, 605, 609; A. Baumeister, *Denkmäler der classischen Alterthum*, p. 1902.

[3] *The Seege of Troye*, etc., vv. 1528–1529; cf. pp. xxxi.–xl.; Granz, *Seege of Troye*, etc., p. 51.

a critical edition of the *Roman de Troie* can we be assured that the two English writers found in their original a suggestion for the change of detail.

It is to be noted that every time "myn auctor" is referred to on a specific point, the *Filostrato* is meant,[1] and if a sonnet of Petrarch,[2] given in a translation[3] in which "nought only the sentence" but "every word" has its equivalent, is attributed to "myn auctor Lollius,"[4] the other reference to that author is upon a detail only found in the work of Boccaccio.[5] Again, in

[1] *T. and C.*, II. 699–791 = *Fil.*, II. 69–75; *T. and C.*, III. 501–504 = *Fil.*, III. 3, 4–5; *T. and C.*, III. 575–578, 568–570 = *Fil.*, III. 21, 4–8; *T. and C.*, III. 1195–1197, cf. *Fil.*, III. 31, 1–3; *T. and C.*, III. 1324–1327 (where Chaucer states that "thogh I can not tellen al, as can myn auctor," after he has taken 126 lines to enlarge upon the substance of 21 lines in the Italian poem, *T. and C.*, III. 1198–1323; cf. *Fil.*, III. 31–33); *T. and C.*, 1814–1817 = *Fil.*, IV. 24, 1–3.   [2] *Sonn.*, 88.   [3] *T. and C.*, I. 400–420.

[4] *T. and C.*, I. 393–399.

[5] *T. and C.*, V. 1653–1673 = *Fil.*, VIII. 8–10; cf. p. 121.

speaking of his poem as a whole, Chaucer only mentions "myn auctor" as his
authority,[1] and three times he makes an
indirect reference to the Italian poem.[2]

When Chaucer states that

"Criseyde was this lady name a-right,"[3]

he accepts the authority of the statement
of Boccaccio, —

"Griseida nomata,"[4]

---

[1] *T. and C.*, I. 260–266, II. 18, 49.

[2] *T. and C.*, I. 492–497 = *Fil.*, I. 48; *T. and C.*, II. 1219–
1225 = *Fil.*, II. 125–127; *T. and C.*, V. 1758–1764 = *Fil.*,
VIII. 26.   [3] *T. and C.*, I. 99.

[4] *Fil.*, I. 11, 6.   Chaucer seems to emphasize the correctness of the change of the name made by Boccaccio,
under the influence of classical authorities, in which the
daughter of the priest Chryses plays such a prominent
part as the captive of Achilles (cf. L. Constans in *Hist.
de la langue et lit. française*, vol. I. p. 209, n.; Hertzberg,
l.c., p. 197), without supposing the additional reason
that "Boccaccio wollte die Chriseis als die Goldige
gedeutet werden" (Hertzberg, *l.c.*, p. 197, accepted by
Koerting, *Boccaccio*, p. 591).   Criseida and Griseida
appeared as the same form in the text of the Italian
poem, as is evident from the fact that both appear in MSS.

rejecting the name " Brisaida," " Briseida," given by the French and Latin writers,[1] although he modified the spelling in later poems to " Creseyde." [2]

Once he refers to a detail in his story, which " writen is in geste," [3] and this proves to be the *Filostrato;* and again, when he states that he is narrating the action of his heroine, —

    " as writen clerkes in hir bokes old,"

of Guido, where the copyists have substituted " Criseida " for " Briseida," the form in the original text. (Morf, *Rom*, vol. XXI. p. 101, n.; cf. Moland et d'Héricault, *l.c.*, p. cxxxv.; Mussafia, *l.c.*, pp. 496–497; Hertzberg, *l.c.*, p. 197.)

[1] *R. de T.*, 12956; *Historia*, sig. i 1. recto, col. 2.

[2] *Against Women Unconstant*, 16; *L. of G. W.*, 332, 441, 469; cf. *H. of F.*, 397–398 : —

    " Eek lo! how fals and reccheles
      Was to Briseida Achilles,"

where the English poet took the classic accusative form as it appeared in Ovid (*Heroides*, III. 137), while in *C. T.*, B, 71, he gives a form, probably of his own making, " Brixseyde "; cf. *Her.*, III. 1, " Briseide."

[3] *T. and C.*, III. 450 = *Fil.*, III. 3, 6.   A satisfactory

he is merely translating a passage from
the Italian poem,[1] which has no parallel
in the other sources.

explanation has not been offered as to what particular
form of narrative is meant by "in geste" in the lines
(*C. T.*, B, 2122–2124):—

> "Sir, at o word, thou shalt no lenger ryme,
>   Let see wher thou canst tellen aught in geste,
>   Or telle in prose somwhat at the leste."

Elsewhere the word, in its meaning of "narrative," refers
indifferently to authorities in Latin verse or prose
(*P. of F.*, 1515; *L. of G. W.*, A, 87; *T. and C.*, II. 83, V.
1511; *C. T.*, B, 1126, D, 642). Gower applies it to
the *T. and C.* (*Mirour de l'omme*, 5253):—

> "U qu'il oït chanter la geste
>   De Troylus et de la belle
>   Creseide."

[1] *T. and C.*, III. 1199 = *Fil.*, III, 32; cf. p. 7;
T. and C., V. 1478–1479:—

> "Of which, as olde bokes tellen us
>   Ther roos a contek and a great envye,"

where Ovid's *Metamorphoses* alone is referred to (cf.
p. 96); and again, *B. of D.*, 52–55:—

> "And in this boke were writen fables
>   That clerkes hadde, in olde tyme
>   And other poets put in ryme,
>   To rede, and for to be in minde."

Once he refers to "the story" for a detail only found in Benoit;[1] and again[2] he calls attention to the same source as the authority for a passage which was necessarily dependent upon the *Roman de Troie*, except for a detail, the hint for which he adopted from the *Filostrato*.[3] In translating the Italian,—

> "Nell' opere opportune alla lor guerra
> Egli era sempre nell' armi il primiero
> Che sopra' Greci uscia fuor della terra,
> Tanto animoso, et si forte e si fiero
> Che ciascun ne dottava, se no erra
> La storia,"[4]

he adds a detail from Benoit,[5] and mentions more than the one authority cited by Boc-

[1] *T. and C.*, V. 1051; cf. p. 124.   [3] Cf. p. 120.
[2] Cf. p. 119, *T. and C.*, V. 1037.   [4] *Fil.*, III. 90.
[5] *R. de T.*, 5418–5420; cf. Constans, *l.c.* p. 63:—

> "De cels de Troie li plus bials
> E li plus prouz, fors que sis frère
> Hector."

In Guido he is always represented as the equal of Hector. See p. 76.

caccio, necessarily including his Italian predecessor as one of his sources: —

"In alle nedes, for the tounes werre,
He was, and ay the firste in armes dight;
And certeynly, but-if that bokes erre,
Save Ector, most y-drad of any wight."[1]

The description of Diomedes is, for the most part, based upon that given in the *Roman de Troie*, with the addition of details from the *Filostrato*, and possibly a hint from Guido,[2] and here Chaucer, in speaking of his authorities, says that the "bokes us declare,"[3] and "some men seyn."[4] Only once, in his description of Troilus, for which he is mainly indebted to Guido's work, does he directly refer to this source, and with the indefinite term, "in storie it

[1] *T. and C.*, III. 1772–1775. [2] Cf. p. 115.
[3] *T. and C.*, V. 799.
[4] *T. and C.*, V. 804; cf. *T. and C.*, I. 708. "Men seyn," where proverb is given, which the "Chanoun yeman," says he, "ones lerned of a clerk," *C. T.*, G, 748; cf. *T. and C.*, II. 1238.

is y-founde." [1]   He mentions "these olde bokes" [2] as his authorities for passages in which he has expanded a line or two in the *Filostrato*, by a statement of events for which he found a detailed account in the works of Benoit and Guido. [3]   If in a passage in which [4] he comments upon Criseyde's actions, the facts could have been furnished by all of his three sources, [5] the kindliness of his reflections upon her motives would on this point exclude the authority of Guido, whom the English poet elsewhere in the poem indirectly rebukes for his harsh opinion of the heroine, —

"Allas! that they shulde ever cause finde
    To speke her harm ; and if they on hir lye,
    Y-wis, hemselfe sholde han the vilanye," [6]

[1] *T. and C.*, V. 834; cf. p. 76.

[2] *T. and C.*, V. 1562, 1753 ; pp. 127–129.   On " olde bokes," cf. pp. 135–136 ; *T. and C.*, V. 1481.

[3] Cf. pp. 111, 127–129.

[4] *T. and C.*, IV. 1415–1421; cf. V. 19–21; cf. pp. 111–112.   [5] *T. and C.*, IV., 15–18; cf. p. 125.

[6] *T. and C.*, IV. 19–21; cf. p. 8, and *C. T.*, F, 551, " as

even if he writes as if he alluded to more than one authority, as he unquestionably does, when he is speaking merely of the facts of the story:—

"Bisechinge every lady bright of hewe,
And every gentil womman, what she be,
That al be that Criseyde was untrewe,
That for that gilt she be not wrooth with me,
Ye may hir gilt in othere bokes see." [1]

"The stories" are the source mentioned for a passage which summarizes a long account in the *Roman de Troie* and the *Historia*.[2] Twice he takes care to mention that certain details are not to be found in his authorities,[3] and if in his delineation of the character of the heroine he writes,—

---

writen folk," where the Biblical narrative seems to be referred to.

[1] *T. and C.*, V. 1772–1776.

[2] *T. and C.*, V. 1044; cf. p. 122; *T. and C.*, V. 1459, "old stories" = "antiche storie," *Fil.*, Proemio, p. 7, *An. and Arc.*, "olde storie," "storia antica," *Tes.*, I. 2.

[3] *T. and C.*, I. 132–133, V. 1086–1092; cf. pp. 82 n., 87.

"But trewely, I can not telle hir age," [1]

he appears to fear to add a specific detail,
which is not elsewhere vouched for.   Yet
in this very passage occurs a bit of characterization which is referred directly to the
authority of those "who writen that her
syen," [2] for which it is difficult to cite what
may be a parallel in any of the sources. [3]
Again, in an episode of the *Troilus* which
had no prototype in the story as told by
the predecessors of the English poet, the
reference is entirely fictitious in the lines —

"But whan his shame gan somwhat to passe
His resons, as I may my rymes holde,
I yow wol telle, as techen bokes olde." [4]

He unquestionably refers to the unnamed
Italian poem as his main authority, and if
he writes of his own poem that

"Out of Latin in my tonge it wryte," [5]

[1] *T. and C.*, V. 826.   [3] Cf. p. 83 n.
[2] *T. and C.*, V. 816.   [4] *T. and C.*, III. 89–91.
        [5] *T. and C.*, II. 1

it was in order to give to his source the dignity that he wished to attribute to that of *Anelida and Arcite*, where, in making a very free translation of a passage in the *Tesaide*,[1] he notes his intention, —

> "in English for tendyte
> This olde storie, in Latin which I fynde,"[2]

when, in fact, he is only using the words of the Italian poem, which treats of something else.[3] And, in the one poem he adopts hints from the *Historia*, which was the Latin source of the *Filostrato*, as in the other he translated passages from Sta-

---

[1] *Tes.*, I. 2 : —

> " Chè m' e venuta voglia com pietosa
> Rima di scriver una storia antica,
> Tanto negli anni riposta e nascosa
> Che latino autor non par ne dica
> Per quel ch' io senta, in libro alcuna cosa."

[2] *An. and Arc.*, 9–10.

[3] Cf. pp. 23–24; ten Brink, *Chaucer*, pp. 49, 53–56; Skeat, *Minor Poems*, p. 311; Koch., *Eng. Stud.*, vol. XV. p. 399.

tius,[1] in whose work Boccaccio found suggestions for the story of the *Tesaide;* so
that he may have felt a right in both cases
to refer to the Latin sources of his Italian
originals as his own. It is to mystify his
readers once more, in order to hide the
name of his author, that he introduces the
name of Lollius, to whom he attributed a
history of the Trojan war,[2] by a misinterpretation of the lines of Horace,[3] which he
found cited in the *Polycraticus* [4] of John of
Salisbury, a work with which he was well
acquainted.[5] For elsewhere he translates
another line of Horace,[6] cited in the same

[1] *An. and Arc.,* 22–48; *Thebias,* XII. 519 ff.; cf. Skeat,
Chaucer's Minor Poems, pp. lxix., 313.

[2] *H. of F.* 1468; cf. p. 51.

[3] *Ep.* l. 2, 1 ff.; cf. pp. 38–40, 46.

[4] *Polycr.,* VII. 9; Migne, *Patrologia,* vol. CXCIX. vol.
657. This passage has already been noted by W. E. A.
Axon, *N. and Q.,* Ser. 9, vol. III. p. 224.

[5] Cf. W. W. Woolcombe in *Essays on Chaucer,* pp. 293–
306; Lounsbury, *Studies in Chaucer,* vol. II. pp. 362–364.

[6] *Ep.,* l. 10, 24 = *C. T.,* H. 161.

work,[1] *à propos* of the matter he is treating
of, again he refers to it by inference as an
authority,[2] and quotes from it a number of
times without mentioning his source.[3] In
the same way in *Anelida and Arcite*, where
he equally avoids mention of Boccaccio, he
avails himself of the name of Corinna, a
contemporary of Pindar, who had been
remembered down to Chaucer's day, as
the author of a work upon the Theban

[1] *Polycr.*, III. 8, col. 489.

[2] *C. T.*, D. 1510–1511; cf. *Polycr.*, II. 27, col. 468;
Woolcombe, *l.c.* p. 295.

[3] *C. T.*, C. 591, 595, 603, 621 = *Polycr.*, I. 5; cols. 399–
400.　On " Stilbon-Chilon," cf. E. Koeppel, *Anglia*, vol.
XIII. p. 183; K. O. Petersen, *On the Sources of the Nonne
Prestes Tale*, p. 100, n.　*C. T.*, H. 226 ff. = *Polycr.*, III. 14;
cf. Petersen, *l.c.* p. 114, n. 1 (Alexander and the pirate);
possibly *C.*, 538 ff. = *Polycr.*, VIII. 6, col. 725; cf. Woolcombe, *l.c.* p. 296; and *Former Age*, 33–40 = *Polycr.*, VIII.
6, col. 727; cf. *Works of Chaucer*, vol. I. p. 541.　On *C. T.*,
C. 517 ff., 527 ff., cf. Woolcombe, *l.c.* pp. 297–304; *Works
of Chaucer*, vol. V. pp. 278–279; Lounsbury, *l.c.* pp. 364–
372.　In the *B. of D.*, 663–664, the information from the
Polycr., I. 5, col. 399, is at second hand, the immediate
source being the *Rom. de la Rose*, 7425 ff.

story, making her with Statius the joint
authorities of his poem,[2] the source of a
large part of which has not been pointed
out.

When he introduces into his narrative

[1] As to the author referred to, I adopt the hint given
by Tyrwhitt, who thinks it hardly possible that Chaucer
"had met with that poem" (*Works of Chaucer*, p. 461).
The mere statement about the composition of the work
could have been as accessible to Chaucer as that about
Agathon, to whom he refers in another poem (*L. of G.
W.*, 525–526; cf. Cary's Dante, note to *Purg.*, XXII. 106;
Bech., *Anglia*, vol. V. p. 365; Skeat, *Legend of Good
Women*, pp. xxiv.–xxvi., 149) in some mediæval encyclo-
pedic work.   Constans (*Roman de Thebes*, vol. II. p. clvii.,
n. 2), who does not know of Chaucer's indebtedness to
Boccaccio in the *Anelida and Arcite*, unnecessarily sug-
gests that Chaucer may have been acquainted with a
Latin translation or abridgment of Corinna's poem,
though he regards it as more probable that her name, as
that of Lollius, was used to conceal the true source.
Hertzberg's suggestion (*Jahr. f. rom. und engl. Lit.*, vol.
VIII. p. 160; *Shak. Jahr.*, vol. VI. pp. 173–174; cf. Skeat,
Chaucer's Minor Poems, p. 312), that Corinnus, a historian
of the Trojan war is referred to, has not as good ground
for acceptance.

[2] *An. and Arc.*, 21 : —

    "First follow I Stace, and after him Corinne."

L

the translation of a sonnet of Petrarch, as a song found in the text of his original, he may have confused the two Italian poets owing to the fact that the authorship of the *Filostrato* in his manuscript, as in that used by the French translator, was attributed to Petrarch;[1] but the very innovation rather denotes that it was done to sustain the mystery with which he wished to surround the origin of his poem, and to avoid here, or elsewhere, mention of Boccaccio, who has been his most important authority throughout all his works.[2]

[1] Cf. pp. 32–33.

[2] In the *Monkes Tale* in the account of Zenobia, for which he drew the material from Boccaccio's *De Casibus Virorum* (VIII. 6) and *De Mulieribus* (ch. xcviii.), if any reader desires details, he writes (*C. T.*, B, 3515–3516) : —

> "Let him un-to my maister Petrark go,
> That writ y-nough of this I undertake."

Tyrwhitt (note to *C. T.*, 14253, *Works of Chaucer*, p. 203) conjectured that "Boccaccio's book had fallen into Chaucer's hand under the name of Petrarch."

He nowhere mentions or even indirectly suggests [1] the title of the *Filostrato* in the *Troilus,* while in the *Knightes Tale,* [2] having in mind the symbolical meaning attributed to the name by Boccaccio, [3] he has one of his characters assume it instead of the name found in the *Tesaide.* [4]   When Chaucer has been at so much pains to conceal the name, the author, and the language of the work which was his main authority, it is not at all surprising that he does not cite by name Benoit or Guido.   To them he merely refers

---

[1] The variant of *T. and C.,* III. 503, found in *St. John's College, Cambridge,* MS., l. 1,

"An hondred vers of which hym liste nat write,"
is the only suggestion of the metrical structure of the original.

[2] *C. T.,* A, 1428, "Philostrato he seide that he heighte." Cf. 1558, 1728.

[3] Cf. p. 95 n.

[4] *Tesaide,* IV. 3, has "Pentheo."   It is to be noted that certain lines of the *Filostrato* that are translated in the *Troilus* reappear in the *Knightes Tale.*   Cf. *C. T.,* A, 1010, 1101, 1163–1168; *T. and C.,* IV. 627; I. 425; IV. 618.

in general terms as authorities for incidents in his story and details in his description of the characters, not found in his Italian original. From their narratives he also borrows, without notice, material for the enlargement of his own story, independent of that of Boccaccio, but taken from the same places in these works, to which the Italian poet had resort. The suggestions taken from the French poem or its Latin plagiary — and often it is a word, a phrase, borrowed from one, sometimes, to supplement the statement of the other — are skilfully introduced into the main texture of the story, in different parts of the *Troilus*.[1] Some of these additions form an essential

---

[1] In the same way Gower inserts details taken from Benoit or Guido into his versions of incidents, the main body of which is borrowed from one of these authors, so that it is sometimes difficult to decide to which one he refers as an authority in the phrases "cronique," "the tale of Troie," "bok of Troie." Cf. *Traitié*, IX. 4; *Conf. Amant.*, III. 2641; V. 3192; I. 483; V. 3244; VII. 1559.

part of his own story, as he first wrote it; others, again, are changes in details of statements, taken from Boccaccio, which he made in revising his poem.[1]

As authorities for the history of the Trojan war, he mentions Homer, Dictys, and Dares,[2] as he found them cited in the *Roman de Troie* and the *Historia Trojana*,[3]

[1] As is shown by the variant readings of *Harleian* MS. 1239.

[2] Cf. p. 12.

[3] Cf. pp. 51 ff.   The stanza (V. 1786–1792),

"Go litel boke, go litel myn tragedye,
   Ther God thy makere yet er that he dye
   So sende myght to make in some comedye
   But litel book no makynge thow nenvye,
   But subgit be to alle poesye
   And kys the steppes where as thow seest space
   Virgile, Ovyde, Omer, Lucan, and Stace,"

is an imitation of the closing lines of the *Thebaid* of Statius (XII. 816–819),

"Vive, precor; nec tu divinam Aeneida tempta,
   Sed longe sequere et vestigia semper adora.
   Mox, tibi si quis adhuc praetendit nubila livor,
   Occidet, et meriti post me referentur honores."

And the last line is merely a variant of the stock formula,

since he was acquainted with only the work of Dares at first hand. In doing this he merely follows the precedent established by mediæval writers, according to which the statements of a translator were as authoritative as those of his original, and a citation at twentieth hand as good as one at first hand. He refers to Dares as an authority upon the warlike exploits of Troilus, and he may well be citing here at first hand.[1]

In his account of Hercules, Chaucer refers to Guido as an authority under the name of Trophee,[2] a translation of his second name "de Columpnis."[3] For the fact that the "columne Herculis" was set up as a token

---

so much used by mediæval poets, in which the greatest writers of antiquity are grouped together. Cf., *e.g.*, F. Michel, *Tristan*, vol. I. p. lxv.; *Romania*, vol. XXV. p. 503; Dante, *Inf.*, IV. 85 ff.

[1] On Chaucer's use of Dares, cf. pp. 59, 61, n. 2, 75 n., 82 n., 130 n.

[2] Cf. p. 55.   [3] Cf. *H. of F.*, 1469, p. 51.

of victory — a trophaeum, trophée[1] — is emphasized by the author of the *Historia,* in the passage translated by the English poet,[2] and elsewhere.[3] Chaucer considers the explanation of Melibee, " that is to seyn, a man that drinketh hony," [4] and the absurd etymologies of the name Cecilia[5] as satisfactory, and so, " to seye in English," this Latin name, makes use of a single word which at once defines and translates it.

[1] Cf. p. 37 ; *Works of Chaucer,* vol. II. p. lvi., n. 1.

[2] Cf. pp. 55–57.

[3] *Historia,* sig. f 5 recto, col. 1. In this passage, evidently as a comment on his own name, Guido speaks of certain so-called " Columne Herculis," situated in the southern part of Italy, which, according to tradition, were put up by the hero in commemoration of his conquest there. On their site, according to Guido, the town of Terranova was built by Frederick II. Cf. *Works of Chaucer,* vol. II. p. lvi., n. 1; *Works of Gower,* ed. G. C. Macaulay, vol. II. p. 501 ; Torraca, *Studi su la lirica italiana del Duecento,* pp. 412–416. It is conceivable that Chaucer referred to these columns, which he may have regarded as being at one of the " worldes endes."

[4] *C. T.,* B, 2599.   [5] *C. T.,* G, 85 ff.

Lydgate finding Trophee cited by Chaucer on the adventures of Hercules, of which Guido gives a similar account,[1] noticing that the treatment of the story of Troilus and Criseyde in the English poem differs from that in the *Historia*,[2] supposes Chaucer's source for both these episodes to be a work in Italian.[3] He himself was not

[1] In Lydgate's translation there seems to be reminiscences of the lines in the *Monkes Tale*. (Troy-book, sig. B 6 recto, col. 1; cf. *Works of Chaucer*, vol. II. p. lv.)

[2] Cf. 15, 75 n., 89 n., 115 n.; *Works of Chaucer*, vol. II. p. 503. On Lydgate's intimate acquaintance with the *Troilus*, cf. J. Schick, *Lydgate's Temple of Glass*, p. cxxvi. *The Gest Hystoriale* omits details in the account of the lovers, because,

"Who-so wilnes to wit of thaire wo fir,
    Turne hym to Troilus and talke there ynoghe."

(8053–8054; cf. *Works of Chaucer*, vol. II. p. lxvi.) Gower, who made use of the works of both Benoit and Guido, always refers to the story as it is found in Chaucer's poem. (*Conf. Amant.*, II. 2457–2459; IV. 2795; V. 7597–7602; VIII. 2531; *Mirour de l'omme*, 5253–5355; *Balades*, XX. 19–22.)

[3] Cf. p. 13.

acquainted with that language,[1] while Chaucer refers to Dante[2] and Petrarch[3] as authorities in the same *Tale* in which he cites from Trophee.   He knows that Chaucer was acquainted with the work of Guido,[4] and accepts his authority as to the existence

[1] Bale's statements that Lydgate had travelled in Italy for the sake of learning the language, that Dante was one of the authors most studied by him, and that he translated some of his writings, as well as some of Petrarch's, have been shown to be worthless; with how-ever much faith they were accepted and enlarged upon by the bibliographers and historians of early English history. (Bale, *Scriptorum illustrium majoris Britanniae Catalogus*, Bâle, 1559, pp. 586, 587 ; Tanner, *Bibliotheca Britannico-Hibernica*, 1748, p. 489; Warton, *History of English Poetry*, 1824, vol. II. p. 362 ; Ritson, *Bibliographia Poetica*, p. 6 ; A. Hortis, *Studi sulle opere latine del Boccaccio*, pp. 627 n., 646–647 ; Constans, *La légende d'Oedipe*, pp. 366–367 ; *Roman de Thèbes*, vol. II. p. clxi; Morley, *English Writers*, vol. VI. p. 103 ; E. Koeppel, *Laurents und Lydgates Bearbeitungen, etc.*, p. 83 ; *Zeit. für vergleichendes Literatur*, vol. I. p. 426 ; Schick, *as cited*, pp. lxxxviii.–xc., xcvi., clii.)

[2] *C. T.*, B, 3657 ; cf. p. 29 n.

[3] *C. T.*, B, 3515 ; cf. p. 145, n. 2.

[4] He makes use of the *Legend of Good Women* in his account of Jason and Medea; cf. pp. 51–53, 53 n.

of a writer upon the Trojan war, named Lollius,[1] although non-committal as to his authorship of the "Trophe." But he has no idea of the real name of the Italian work of which he speaks, or of its author, his favorite Boccaccio.

[1] Cf. pp. 14–15.

ADDITIONS AND CORRECTIONS

By an oversight I have failed to note **G. C. Macaulay's** contributions. In a communication to the *Academy* of April 6, 1895, he maintained the theory that the work of Guido was not used at all in the *Troilus*, as Chaucer is really indebted to Benoit in those passages in the English poem for which there seems to be analogues in the *Historia*. In a note in **F. J.** Furnivall's *Three More Parallel Texts of Chaucer's Troilus and Criseyde*, pp. a–b, he cites a number of passages from the *Roman de Troie*, which were unquestionably the original of some lines of Chaucer, and notes that only in the fifth book is use made of this auxiliary source. By the same slip I have overlooked the edition of *Harleian* MS., 1239, an indifferent copy of an early version of the *Troilus*, from which I have only cited at second-hand, and without due emphasis. The readings cited below, for the most part are not found in the other MSS., but it may be grouped on account of other characteristics, with *Cambridge Univ. Libr.* MS. Gg. 4. 27, and *St. John's College, Cambridge*, MS. L 1.

P. 7. The variant of *T. and C.*, III. 1327 (*Harl.* and *St. John's*), —

" In every thing the gret(e) of his sentence,"

modifies the statement regarding the fidelity with which the original is reproduced,

and it is to be noted that this explanation
is in a passage that is found in a different
place in the other MSS.

Pp. 8, 122.   *T. and C.*, V. 1044 : —

"I fynde eke in the story elles where."

The correct plural form, "stories," in the
revised version refers to both the French
and Latin sources, while in lines 1037,
1051, only Benoit needs to be referred to
as an authority.

P. 73.   With *T. and C.*, I. 293–298, cf.
II. 533–535, 902.

Pp. 74, 100, 109–110.   *T. and C.*, IV.
1411.   The reading, —

"Whan he from Delphos, to the grekys sterte,"

adds a detail of the story as it is found in
Benoit and Guido.

P. 81.   *R. de Tr.*, 5231 has the variant : —

"Mais ces sorcilles li joignoient."

P. 83.   With *T. and C.*, V. 1004, cf. III.
1164.

P. 90, n. *T. and C.*, V. 1558 : —

" For as he drow a kynge by the ventaille."

P. 101. *T. and C.*, IV. 50–56 : —

" At whiche day was taken Antenor,
  Palidomas and also Menestes,
  Santipe, Sarpedon, Polinestor,
  Polite and eke the Troian dan Ruphes,
  And other lee folk as Phebuosos,
  For al Ector, so that the folk of Troye
  Drede the lese a gret part of hir Ioye."

This is evidently a bad copy of a version of the stanza in the Filostrato, in which the inconsistency noted had not been corrected.

P. 102. The reading of *T. and C.*, IV. 57–59, —

" To Pryamus whas yeven at his requeste
  A tyme of trew,"

is again the uncorrected version of the original.

P. 105, n. 2. The reading of *T. and C.*, IV. 137–138, in *Harl.* 1239 is a translation of a line of Boccaccio, in which the later version makes a change, not altogether happy, by the addition of a detail found in the other sources.

P. 109, n.   In a note to Gower's *Conf. Amant.*, V. 7451–7455, —

> "This, which Cassandre thanne hihte,
> In al the world as it berth sihte,
> In bokes as men finde write,
> Is that Sibille of whom you wite,
> That alle men yit clepen sage,"

Macaulay refers to, but does not cite a passage in the *Pantheon* of Godfrey of Viterbo, which shows that in Chaucer's lines there is a misunderstanding of a prevalent mediæval tradition. Godfrey is treating of the various sibyls, and of these he tells us, "Fuit igitur haec Sibylla Priami regis filia, et ex matre Hecuba procreata. Vocata est autem in Graeco Tiburtina; Latine vero Albunea nomine, vel Cassandra." *Pantheon*, Pars X, in Pistorius, *Scriptores de Rebus Germanicis*, vol. II. p. 157; cf. *Works of Gower*, vol. III. p. 510.

P. 112. *T. and C.*, IV. 1421 : —

" Thus wryten thoo that ever the Iestes knew."

P. 116, n. 1. Kittredge (*Observations*, etc., pp. 410, 412, 418) notes the verses which are metrically defective in some or all the MSS.

Pp. 119–120, n. The variant of *T. and C.*, V. 1039, —

" The wych of hym whan Troylus,"

suggests an episode of which I cannot state the source.

P. 121. *R. de Tr.*, 15102–15104 : —

" La destre manche de son braz
Bone et fresche de ciclaton,
Li done en leu de gonfanon."

P. 125. *T. and C.*, V. 1095 : —

" Hir name, allas ! ys punysshed so wyde."

P. 130. *T. and C.*, V. 1806 (*Harl.* 1239 and 3943 ; *St. John's*) : —

" Ful pitously hym slough the fiers(e)
Ac(c)hille."